THE WEB WIZARD'S GUIDE TO JAVASCRIPT

STEVEN ESTRELLA

Addison
Wesley

Boston San Francisco New York
London Toronto Sydney Tokyo Singapore Madrid
Mexico City Munich Paris Cape Town Hong Kong Montreal

Executive Editor: *Susan Hartman Sullivan*
Associate Managing Editor: *Pat Mahtani*
Executive Marketing Manager: *Michael Hirsch*
Production Supervision: *Diane Freed*
Cover and Interior Designer: *Leslie Haimes*
Composition: *Gillian Hall, The Aardvark Group*
Copyeditor: *Betsy Hardinger*
Proofreader: *Holly McLean-Aldis*
Cover Design: *Gina Hagen Kolenda*
Prepress and Manufacturing: *Caroline Fell*

Access the latest information about Addison-Wesley titles from our World Wide Web site: *http://www.aw.com/cs*

Library of Congress Cataloging-in-Publication Data
Estrella, Steven G.
      The Web Wizard's guide to JavaScript / Steven G. Estrella.
         p. cm.
      Includes bibliographical references and index.
      ISBN 0-201-75833-4(pbk.)
      1. JavaScript (Copmuter program language) I. Title.

      QA76.73J39 E88 2002
      005.2'762--dc21
                                     2001045798
                                     CIP

2345678910—QWT—04030201

Books are to be returned on or before
the last date below.

THE
WEB W
GUIDE
JAVAS

- 3 FEB 2003

07 MAY 2003

2 3 SEP 2005

JOHN
TITH
LIVERPOOL L2 2
TEL. 0151 231 4022

LIBREX —

TABLE OF CONTENTS

PREFACE

About Addison-Wesley's Web Wizard Series

The beauty of the Web is that, with a little effort, anyone can harness its power to create sophisticated Web sites. Addison-Wesley's Web Wizard Series helps students master the Web by presenting a concise introduction to one important Internet topic or technology in each book. The books start from square one and assume no prior experience with the technology being covered. Mastering the Web doesn't come with a wave of a magic wand; but by studying these accessible, highly visual textbooks, readers will be well on their way.

The series is written by instructors who are familiar with the challenges beginners face when learning the material. To this end, the Web Wizard books offer more than a cookbook approach: they emphasize principles and offer clear explanations, giving the reader a strong foundation of knowledge on which to build.

Numerous features highlight important points and aid in learning:

☆ Tips — important points to keep in mind

☆ Shortcuts — timesaving ideas

☆ Warnings — things to watch out for

☆ Do It Yourself — activities to try now

☆ Review questions and hands-on exercises

☆ Online references — Web sites to visit to obtain more information

Supplementary materials for the books, including updates, additional examples, and source code, are available at `http://www.aw.com/webwizard`. Also available for qualified instructors adopting a book from the series are instructor's manuals, sample tests, and solutions. Please contact your Addison-Wesley sales representative for the instructor resources password.

About This Book

When I first began developing Web sites way back in 1994, I was grateful to be able to display a simple graphic or add bold to my text. The Web was a static medium in those days. Interactivity was limited to the links you created to navigate from one page to another. Web designers had little control over how their content would appear. Media elements other than text and simple graphics were rarely used due to bandwidth limitations and lack of standards. The most popular background color for a Web page back then was gray. My, how things have changed.

Today's Web sites are highly interactive and rich in media content. JavaScript plays a large role in the development of contemporary Web sites because it offers a relatively easy way to interact with the objects that Web browsers create. As a result, Web designers no longer view their creations as a series of static pages linked together by navigation icons. Instead, Web designers create environments where visitors interact with text, graphics, animation, sound, and video. The visitor is an active participant rather than a passive recipient.

This book will introduce you to the fundamentals of the JavaScript language and help you learn to visualize the interaction of objects in a Web browser environment. A solid grounding in HTML 4 is recommended before studying JavaScript. The concepts and skills you learn here will take your HTML code to the next level. You will learn to manipulate the content of your Web page both before and after the page loads. You will learn how to gather information from your visitors to customize their Web browsing experiences. You will gain a solid understanding of a language that has changed the nature of the Internet.

Acknowledgments

No book is produced by one person. I would like to extend my thanks to my editors Elinor Actipis and Susan Hartman Sullivan for their encouragement—and for the wonderful chocolate desserts. Thanks go to my industrious and alert copy editor, Betsy Hardinger, and to Gillian Hall for her creative typesetting. Many thanks go to Diane Freed for her humor and diligence in keeping everyone on schedule. In addition, the book reviewers offered many excellent ideas and changes, which truly made this a better book. These reviewers include

John Hollenbeck, San Francisco State University
Donna Occhifinto, County College of Morris
Carla Gesell-Streeter, Cincinnati State Technical and Community College
Robert N. Barger, University of Notre Dame
James A. White, Ph.D., University of South Florida
Tammy Ashley, New Hampshire Community Technical College–Manchester
Don Anderson, Chadron State College.

My apologies to my pet corgi, Clara Belle, whose frisbee needs unfortunately were neglected during the writing of this book. Most of all, I extend my thanks and admiration to my best friend and wife, Kathleen Schietroma, whose persistence and focus continue to inspire me.

Steven Estrella
September 2001

CHAPTER ONE

JavaScript Basics

Y ou're probably reading this book because you know how to create Web pages with Hypertext Markup Language (HTML) and now you want to make your pages more interesting and dynamic. This book will help you get started by providing clear explanations of the fundamentals of the JavaScript language together with code examples to demonstrate key concepts.

Chapter Objectives

- To discover the many good reasons to learn JavaScript
- To learn the history of JavaScript
- To master fundamental concepts: objects, properties, values, methods, events, variables, arrays, and functions
- To become familiar with the Document Object Model

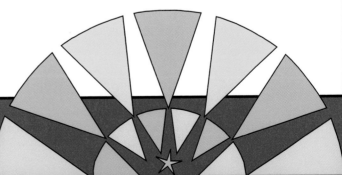

⊚◎ Why Learn JavaScript?

JavaScript is a scripting language designed for the Web. You integrate JavaScript code directly into HTML documents, and your visitors' Web browsers interpret the code when they load the document. JavaScript's main claim to fame is that it allows Web developers to include high levels of interactivity in Web pages.

There are many great reasons for learning JavaScript.

☆ Virtually all Web browsers support JavaScript.

☆ JavaScript is a very popular language. As a result, hundreds of scripts are available for download at JavaScript sites. You can learn from the work of others.

☆ An increasing number of multimedia authoring programs, such as Macromedia Flash and Macromedia Director, rely on JavaScript or JavaScript-like languages to create interactivity and enhance interfaces.

☆ JavaScript lets you use external code libraries (`.js` files), encouraging reusable code.

☆ The syntax of JavaScript is very similar to the syntax of C, C++, and Java. The time you invest in learning JavaScript will bear fruit for years to come.

☆ Learning a programming language is good for the mind. To succeed in programming, you must use creative problem solving and logical thinking. The study of programming encourages you to develop these abilities.

⊚◎ A Little History

Originally called LiveScript, JavaScript was invented by Brendan Eich at Netscape in 1995. Netscape and Sun Microsystems worked together to include JavaScript in the Netscape Navigator 2.0 Web browser. The name change capitalized on the marketing hype surrounding Sun's Java language.

☆**WARNING** JavaScript is not Java! The languages are similar in appearance and structure, but Java is a full-featured, structured programming language similar in scope to C or C++. JavaScript, on the other hand, is a small scripting language designed to enhance Web pages. The most relevant difference for you is that JavaScript is much easier to learn.

JavaScript's popularity increased with the introduction of Netscape Navigator 3.0. Web page authors began to include image swapping, scrolling text in the status bar, form validation, and other dynamic effects. Shortly thereafter, Microsoft's Internet Explorer 3.0 introduced a competing language, JScript, which was almost identical to the original LiveScript language. The differences between JavaScript and JScript are largely inconsequential. Both are scripting languages. Scripts in the theater world direct the actions of players on a stage. **Scripts** in the Web world direct the behavior of **objects** (documents, images, forms, etc.) loaded in a Web browser's window. Unfortunately, these objects were organized very differently in Netscape Navigator 3 and Internet Explorer 3. As a result, the procedures for using JScript in Internet Explorer were different from the procedures for using JavaScript in Netscape Navigator. As the browsers developed, the languages began to diverge to accommodate the different **object models** of the two browsers.

A European computer standards group known only as ECMA (pronounced "Eckma") worked with Netscape and Microsoft to produce a standard scripting language called ECMAScript in 1997. Both Netscape Communicator 4 and Internet Explorer 4 implemented ECMAScript as the foundation for the latest versions of JavaScript and JScript. Using ECMA and a little creativity, Web authors gradually developed programming practices that worked equally well with the object models of both browsers. Those are the practices that you'll learn in this book.

⊚⊚ Fundamental Concepts of JavaScript

As you read the following overview of JavaScript concepts and vocabulary, keep in mind that it's an introductory reference. The first time each concept or term appears in subsequent chapters, it will be explained in more detail. For now, review this section to get an overview of the language.

> ☆**TIP**   The Web site for this book contains an interactive version of this overview to assist you in understanding the concepts. Visit `http://www.awl.com/estrella`.

Objects

An **object** is any definable thing. A car is one example of an object in the physical world. A car may contain other objects, such as a trunk. In turn, the trunk may contain other objects, such as a spare tire.

JavaScript is an **object-oriented** language. In JavaScript, a **hierarchy** of objects is represented in code using **dot syntax**. For example, here's how you might use dot syntax to represent a spare tire:

```
car.trunk.sparetire
```

In JavaScript, a Web browser window and a currently loaded HTML document are examples of common objects created by the host environment (i.e., the Web browser itself). The window contains the document, and the document may contain other objects, such as images, forms, buttons, and links. In JavaScript, every object can be given a name and referred to in the code using dot syntax. Here's an example (illustrated in Figure 1.1):

```
window.document.gardendog
```

> ☆**TIP**   Think of objects as the nouns of the JavaScript language.

The code for this window would refer to an image named "gardendog" in a document loaded in a Web browser window.

Figure 1.1 An Image Object in a Web Browser Window

Instance

An **instance** is one particular incarnation of an object. For example, a car is an object, and the Beetle parked across the street is one instance of the car object. An instance of an object inherits all the characteristics of the object type. For example, if a car always has a trunk and a spare tire, any instance of the car object, including my neighbor's Beetle, can be assumed to have these items.

`Beetle.trunk.sparetire` would be the code used to designate the spare tire in the trunk of a Beetle (one instance of the more generic car object).

In the same way, a photograph named "gardendog" loaded in a Web page is one instance of the more generic image object.

Properties

In real life, instances of objects can also have **properties**. An instance of the car object might have a property known as color. That property would be referred to in JavaScript as

`Beetle.color`

Similarly, in the JavaScript language, each object can have many associated properties. For example, the document object has a built-in property called bgColor (note the use of both upper- and lowercase letters) that represents the background color:

```
window.document.bgColor
```

Values

In real life, properties have **values**. A car object may have a property known as color with a value known as blue. If the owner of a Beetle (an instance of the car object) paints the car a different color, he would assign a new value to the color property. The following code assigns the value red to the property color of the car object instance Beetle:

```
Beetle.color="red";
```

JavaScript objects also have properties, and you can assign values to them. For example, the document object has a property called bgColor, which represents the background color and can be assigned a value such as silver using this JavaScript statement:

```
window.document.bgColor="silver";
```

Perhaps the most common use of JavaScript is to create **rollover** graphics, in which the image changes when the viewer moves the mouse over it. This technique relies on the SRC (source) property of the image object in JavaScript. The SRC property has a value to indicate the location and name of a graphics file located on the hard drive of the Web server.

The HTML page in Listing 1.1 presents an image of a woman in a field of sunflowers (see Figure 1.2). The image is created using the standard HTML tag IMG, which has the SRC property. In this example, SRC has the value "sunflowerlady.jpg," which indicates that an image file called "sunflowerlady.jpg" resides in the same folder as the Web page itself. Another property of the IMG tag is the NAME property, which here is set to the value "sunflowerphoto."

```
<html><head><title>sunflower lady</title></head>
<body bgcolor="white">
<img src="sunflowerlady.jpg" width="300"
height="200"  name="sunflowerphoto">
</body>
</html>
```

Listing 1.1 HTML Page with IMG Tag

When this code is included in a Web page and loaded into a window by a Web browser, an instance of the generic image object is created and exists in the memory of the browser under the name sunflowerphoto.

> ☆**TIP**   Notice that JavaScript code statements should end with a semicolon. A **statement** is a single command sent to the JavaScript interpreter in the Web browser. The semicolon tells the JavaScript interpreter where the statement ends.

Figure 1.2 Output of Listing 1.1

JavaScript lets you include code that changes the value of the SRC property of an image object and thereby implement the rollover feature. This means that you can change the image even after the page has been loaded into the browser window. For example, the following code changes the SRC property of the image in Figure 1.2 to show a close-up of the sunflowers (see Figure 1.3):

```
document.sunflowerphoto.src="sunflowers.jpg";
```

Figure 1.3 Close-up of the Sunflowers

That explains how the image is changed. But how does the browser know to change the image only when the viewer rolls the mouse over it? That brings us to the subject of events and event handlers.

Events and Event Handlers

In real life, objects sometimes encounter **events**. An instance of the car object might encounter the blowout event, resulting in a change in the shape of the tire. The tire responds to the event by changing its shape to flat. A JavaScript **event handler** is the code that responds to events initiated by visitors to a Web page. In this example, the blowout event is handled by an `onBlowOut` handler, which responds to the event by changing the value of the `shape` property of the tire object:

```
onBlowOut=Beetle.tire.shape="flat";
```

Similarly, JavaScript objects encounter many events. One of the most common events is the **mouseover** event triggered when a visitor moves the mouse on top of an object. The anchor tag (`<a>`) can be set to respond to mouseover events. Any text or graphics enclosed by an anchor tag can then be used to trigger the mouseover event.

In the following example, a **link** (the `<a>` tag) is coded with the `onmouseover` handler to change the background color of the page to silver when the visitor moves the mouse over the link. The HREF property is set to "#" so that nothing happens if the user clicks the link.

```
<a href="#" onmouseover="document.bgColor='silver';">
Roll over to change background to silver.</a>
```

To implement the **image swap**, you use an IMG tag in place of the text. Listing 1.2 sets up a rollover graphic. When the user moves the mouse over the image of the sunflower lady, a mouseover event is generated. The anchor tag has an event handler `onmouseover` to handle the mouseover event. The event handler sends a single line of code to the browser to change the SRC property of the "sunflower-photo" image to display the close-up of the sunflowers. An `onmouseout` event handler restores the original image when the mouse is no longer on top of the image.

Read the code in Listing 1.2. You may be surprised at how much you understand even this early in your study of JavaScript.

☆ **SHORTCUT** You will learn about image swapping in greater detail in Chapters Four and Five. To create Listing 1.2 yourself, download the two images from `http://www.awl.com/estrella/`, type the code into any text editor, save it as a plain text file with the file name extension `.html`, and open it in your Web browser.

☆ **TIP** In the code listings, the symbol ¬ indicates a line of text that wraps (runs over) to the next line because of the line length limitations of the printed page (see the code at the top of the next page). It's important to avoid placing unnecessary carriage returns in your code. A JavaScript statement with a carriage return in the middle won't work properly in the Web browser.

```
<html><head><title>sunflower image swap</title></head>
<body bgcolor="white">
<a href="#" onmouseover="document.sunflowerphoto.src = ¬
'sunflowers.jpg';"
onmouseout="document.sunflowerphoto.src = ¬
'sunflowerlady.jpg';">
<img src="sunflowerlady.jpg" width="300" height="200" ¬
name="sunflowerphoto" border="0"></a>
</body>
</html>
```

Listing 1.2 Image Swapping

☆**TIP**   JavaScript portions of the code
listings in this book appear in blue.

☆**WARNING** **Be Sensitive!**

When you learned HTML, you were probably relieved to discover that HTML tags are not case-sensitive. `<IMG>` and `<img>` are the same in HTML. JavaScript, however, is case-sensitive. In the current example, "sunflowerphoto" and "SunflowerPhoto" are not equivalent. As you name objects and refer to them in JavaScript code, be aware of uppercase and lowercase letters.

Variables

In real life, we deal with **variables** all the time. At a diner, several regular customers may order "the usual." The food server, being familiar with each patron, assigns the value "ham and cheese" to the variable "the usual" for one patron, and assigns the value "veggie burger" to the variable "the usual" for another patron. In this case, the scope of the variable is **local**. It is valid only at a particular diner. If the patron goes to a new diner and requests "the usual," the food server will not understand. A **global** variable, on the other hand, would be understood in every restaurant in the world. An example of a global variable is "the check"; every food server understands that each customer must pay for the food.

When a variable contains a value, you can assign that value to the property of an object. The following code illustrates the creation and use of a variable to assign the color teal to the Beetle instance of the car object. Notice that the `var` keyword is used to **initialize** (that is, to create) a variable.

```
var myFavoriteColor = "teal";
Beetle.color = myFavoriteColor;
```

Similarly, in JavaScript, the value for a property such as bgColor can be placed in a variable:

```
var myBackgroundColor = "silver";
window.document.bgColor = myBackgroundColor;
```

Arrays

An **array** is an ordered collection of data. Each element of an array is a variable and can hold data of any type. You usually use an array to hold related data. An example is an array that represents the nooks in a spice rack. In this case, each element of the array represents a nook. Each nook can contain any spice you might like.

```
Var spicerack = new Array();
spicerack[0] = "oregano";
spicerack[1] = "salt";
spicerack[2] = "pepper";
```

The numbering of the array elements always begins at 0, but sometimes programmers do not populate the [0] element so that numbering can begin more naturally at 1. You can reassign the value of any element in the array by using a statement such as this one:

```
spicerack[0] = "garlic";
```

Arrays are useful because you can change the value of each array element using a programming loop. You will learn about loops in Chapter Two.

Methods

In real life, objects sometimes have actions associated with them. In JavaScript, an object's associated actions are called **methods**. Each generic object has methods associated with it. All instances of the car object, for example, have an associated method called brake that slows the car.

> ☆ **TIP** Think of methods as the verbs in the JavaScript language.

Like variables, methods can take values. For example, the brake method could take values of fast or slow depending on how much force the driver applied to the pedal. In JavaScript, parentheses are used to contain the values associated with a method.

Methods associated with an object are inherited by any instance of that object. A Beetle is an instance of a generic car object. Therefore, the Beetle can use the brake method:

```
Beetle.brake("fast");
Beetle.brake("slow");
```

Often, methods are triggered by events. Suppose our Beetle car object encounters the blowout event. The Beetle must handle this event by performing the brake method. In this example, the blowout event is handled by the onBlowOut event handler, which responds to the event by initiating the brake method:

```
onBlowOut = Beetle.brake('fast');
```

Similarly, Web browser objects have many methods. One of the simplest methods is the write method of the document object. This method is used to write text to the current document as the page loads:

```
document.write("Greetings JavaScript Students");
```

Assignment Operators

To assign a value to a variable, you use a simple assignment operator such as the equal sign ("="):

```
var myAge = 39;
var myName = "Steven";
```

After a value has been assigned, you can alter it using compound operators such as the add-by-value (+=), subtract-by-value (-=), multiply-by-value (*=), and divide-by-value (/=) operators.:

```
var myAge = 39;
myAge += 4; //is the same as myAge = myAge + 4;
            //Result is 43.
myAge -= 4; //is the same as myAge = myAge - 4;
            //Result is 35.
myAge *= 4; //is the same as myAge = myAge * 4;
            //Result is 156.
myAge /= 4; //is the same as myAge = myAge / 4;
            //Result is 9.75.
```

For text values, the addition operator ("+") **concatenates** (joins) text strings together.

```
var myName = "Steven";
myName += " Estrella"; //result is "Steven Estrella"
```

Comparison Operators

Comparison operators let you compare values. The **equality** operator is expressed as two equal signs (==).

> ☆ **WARNING** One of the most common programming errors in JavaScript (and other languages) is to use the assignment operator (=) when you really want the equality operator (==). Use the assignment operator to assign a new value to a variable. Use the equality operator to compare values of two variables.

Statements using comparison operators always result in **Boolean** values (values limited to TRUE or FALSE). **AND** statements comparing two expressions are TRUE if the expressions on both sides of the comparison operator are TRUE. **OR** statements comparing two expressions are TRUE if either expression is TRUE.

```
39 == 30 + 9; //This statement returns a value of TRUE.
39 != 25 + 9; //This statement returns a value of TRUE.
39 > 28; //This statement returns a value of TRUE.
39 >= 39; //This statement returns a value of TRUE.
39 <= 36; //This statement returns a value of FALSE.
(15 == 10+5) && (33 == 28 + 3); //This AND statement
//returns a value of FALSE because one of the
//expressions is false.
```

```
(15 == 10+5) || (33 == 28 + 3); //This OR statement
//returns a value of TRUE because one of the expressions
//is true.
"Red" == "Blue"; //This statement returns a value of
                 //FALSE.
"Red" != "Blue"; //This statement returns a value of
                 //TRUE.
```

Functions

A **function** is a group of JavaScript statements that performs a designated task. Functions are often stored in the HEAD section of an HTML document and do their work when **invoked** (that is, **called**) by other JavaScript statements. A function begins with the word "function" followed by the name of the function and a pair of left and right parentheses. The left and right curly braces, { and }, are used to contain the statements of the function.

```
function doSomething(){
   var theVisitor = document.myform.visitor.value;
   window.alert("Is this OK, " + theVisitor + "?");
}
```

Here is a simple example. The HTML code in Listing 1.3 creates a form that contains a place for the visitor to type a name along with a button to click (see Figure 1.4). When the button is clicked, the doSomething function is called and an **alert box** containing the visitor's name is displayed. The alert box is generated by the alert method of the window object. The alert method takes a value consisting of a string of text plus whatever value was typed into the username field on the Web page plus a question mark. The result is displayed as an alert box.

> ☆**TIP**   You will learn how to write code in detail in Chapter Two, but you may wish to try typing Listing 1.3 just to get your feet wet. Type carefully (spelling counts), or the code won't work.

```
<html><head><title>A Basic Function</title>
<script type="text/javascript" language="JavaScript">
<!-- Hides scripts from really old browsers.
function doSomething(){
   var theVisitor = document.myform.visitor.value;
   window.alert("Is this OK, " + theVisitor + "?");
}
//Ends script hiding -->
</script>
</head>
<body bgcolor="white">
<p>Please type your name and click the button.</p>
<form name="myform">
```

```
<input type="text" size="30" name="visitor"><br><br>
<input type="button" name="mybutton" value="Do Something"
onclick="doSomething();">
</form>
</body>
</html>
```

Listing 1.3 A Web Page with a Simple Function

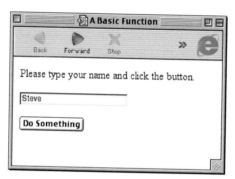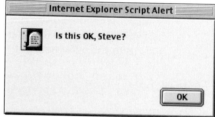

Figure 1.4 Output of Listing 1.3

◎◎ The Document Object Model

Document Object Model (DOM) is a hierarchical model to represent the objects created by a Web browser. In 2000 the World Wide Web Consortium (W3C) published a standard DOM called DOM1. The latest Web browsers, including Netscape 6 and Internet Explorer 5.5, use DOM1. The older browsers, such as Netscape 4 and Internet Explorer 4, use their own proprietary DOMs. As a result, JavaScript programmers must be careful to produce code that works well in all three DOMs. Web page authors historically have spent about 25 percent of their development time dealing with the inconsistencies between the DOMs of the two major browsers. DOM1 now adds a third to the mix.

A DOM is an internal map of all objects found on a Web page (see Figure 1.5). In all current DOMs, the browser window is at the top of the hierarchy. The document object is one level below the window object. Any scriptable objects within the document, such as forms and links, may also have subordinate objects. For example, the text field example in the preceding section is an INPUT object of type TEXT and is called visitor. The visitor object is part of a FORM object called myform, which in turn is part of the current document and window. It is necessary to specify the complete path to any object you wish to manipulate in scripting. Hence, you can use a line of JavaScript code such as this one to alter the value of the visitor object:

```
window.document.myform.visitor.value = "Some text goes
here";
```

In practice, the reference to the current window can be assumed, so programmers often simply type

```
document.myform.visitor.value = "Some text goes here";
```

One of the principal differences between the DOMs of Netscape and Microsoft is the use of the ALL keyword in Microsoft's Internet Explorer. The ALL keyword makes it easier to create references to deeply nested objects in Internet Explorer than in Netscape Communicator. You can reference any uniquely named object in the Internet Explorer DOM using the following structure:

```
document.all.someobjectname;
```

DOM1 establishes a new method for accessing an object on a Web page:

```
document.getElementById(elementID);
```

This works for SPAN and DIV tags or any other object with a unique ID property coded in HTML. Netscape Communicator 6 and Internet Explorer 5.x now support DOM1.

As older browser versions fall into disuse, it may eventually be possible to code pages for compatibility only with DOM1. For now, however, you need to learn techniques that work with all three DOMs. Understanding all the details of the three DOMs takes time and patience. Fortunately, the techniques you will learn in this book have already been tested for compatibility with the three DOMs. Concepts related to the DOMs will be introduced in context as needed.

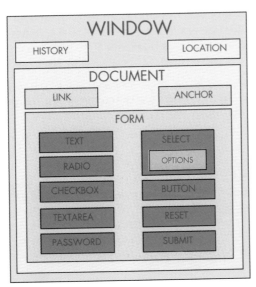

Figure 1.5 Hierarchy of Objects in the Document Object Model

☆ Summary

> JavaScript is a scripting language designed for the Web. It is the most popular and most supported language used today to enhance Web pages.

> Netscape created JavaScript as a proprietary language for its browsers. Today, the language is also known as ECMAScript, a nonproprietary standard developed by a European standards body known as ECMA.

> JavaScript is an object-oriented language. Elements present on Web pages are stored as objects in the memory of the browser. Like objects in the real world, Web browser objects have properties and capabilities. Objects in a Web browser may respond to events like mouseover and click. Event handlers are small pieces of code designed to respond to events. Variables are containers for information. The value held in a variable may be changed using an assignment operator (=). Arrays are ordered collections of data. A spice rack is an array in the real world. Each position in the spice rack may be filled with any spice and the chef may rearrange the spices at any time. Methods are the verbs of the JavaScript language. Methods describe the actions that objects may perform. The most frequent programming error is confusing the assignment operator (=) with the equality operator (==). The assignment operator changes values in a variable. The equality operator is used to compare the values of two variables or expressions. Functions are groups of JavaScript statements that perform a task and often return a value.

> The Document Object Model is an internal map of objects on a Web page. The Netscape and Internet Explorer Web browsers use different DOMs, but the new DOM1, recently published by the W3C, has created a standard DOM for use in future versions of all browsers.

☆ Online References

Netscape's official developer pages for JavaScript.
`http://developer.netscape.com/docs/manuals/javascript.html`

CNET.com's JavaScript tips and tutorials.
`http://builder.cnet.com`

The official W3C page on DOM1.
`http://www.w3.org/TR/REC-DOM-Level-1/`

☆ Review Questions

1. Give an example of an object on a Web page.
2. What is an instance?
3. What is the relationship between properties and values?
4. Explain how to create a rollover image swap.
5. List three examples of variables in your daily life.
6. Describe an example of an array in your daily life.
7. JavaScript methods are associated with what part of speech?
8. Explain the difference between the assignment and equality operators.
9. What is a Boolean value?
10. Describe the structure of a JavaScript function.

☆ Hands-On Exercises

1. Create a Web page with four rollover links to allow visitors to change the background color. Valid named colors for Web page backgrounds are white, black, green, maroon, olive, navy, purple, gray, red, yellow, blue, teal, lime, aqua, fuchsia, and silver. Use the code found in Events and Event Handlers in this chapter.

2. Create a Web page with a rollover image swap. Make sure the two images are exactly the same dimensions.

3. Create a Web page that contains a form having a text input field and a button. Add a function to display an alert when the button is clicked. Make sure the text of the alert box contains the text the user typed.

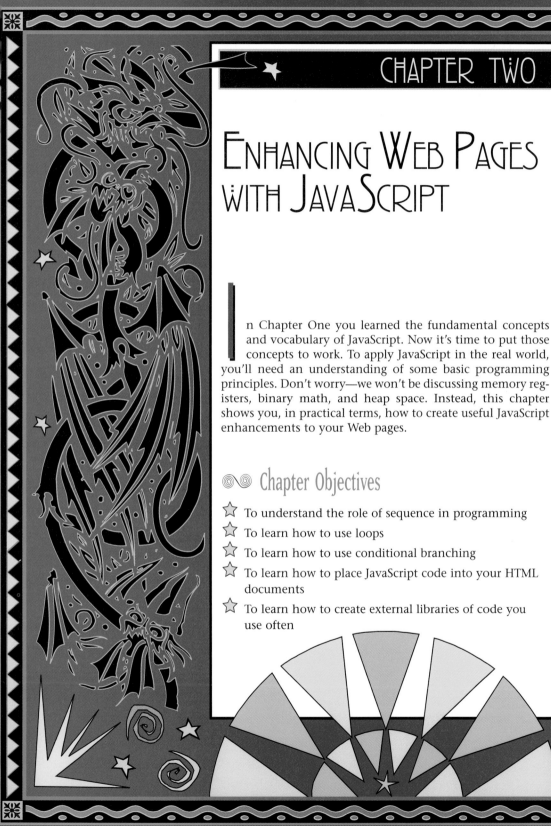

CHAPTER TWO

ENHANCING WEB PAGES WITH JAVASCRIPT

In Chapter One you learned the fundamental concepts and vocabulary of JavaScript. Now it's time to put those concepts to work. To apply JavaScript in the real world, you'll need an understanding of some basic programming principles. Don't worry—we won't be discussing memory registers, binary math, and heap space. Instead, this chapter shows you, in practical terms, how to create useful JavaScript enhancements to your Web pages.

Chapter Objectives

☆ To understand the role of sequence in programming

☆ To learn how to use loops

☆ To learn how to use conditional branching

☆ To learn how to place JavaScript code into your HTML documents

☆ To learn how to create external libraries of code you use often

☆ To learn how to use a Web page that creates other Web pages

☆ To understand how to create a Web page to test your code

◎◎ Sequence: Doing Things in a Given Order

Imagine for a moment that you are the parent of a 13-year-old boy who is beginning to grow facial hair. Let's call him Alex. It's your job to teach Alex how to shave his face. Your explanation might go something like this:

1. Wash your face with a wet cloth.
2. Apply shaving cream to your skin.
3. Scrape a razor blade over your skin to remove facial hair.
4. Apply after-shave lotion to your face.
5. Scream loudly.

> ☆ **TIP**   If you read this chapter while connected to the Internet, you can see all the code examples in action at the book's Web site, `http://www.awl.com/estrella/`.

These five steps represent a **sequence** of instructions. Alex performs instruction 2 only after completing instruction 1 and so on. Similarly, a Web browser performs a series of JavaScript statements in the order it receives them. Unlike Alex, however, your browser doesn't have any intelligence. You must therefore take care to be precise in crafting your instructions.

The sequence of JavaScript statements in Listing 2.1 creates a string of text that is then displayed to the user in an alert box, as shown in Figure 2.1.

The `<script> </script>` tags identify all the statements they enclose as code to be interpreted. The `type = "text/javascript"` attribute identifies the code as JavaScript. The latest browsers (Internet Explorer 5+ and Netscape 6+) recognize the `TYPE` attribute in the `<script>` tag because it is part of the HTML 4.0 specification. Older browsers rely on the `language = "JavaScript"` attribute. To be on the safe side, it's best to include both attributes, as shown in the example.

> ☆ **TIP**   **Care to Comment?**
>
> Placing comments in your JavaScript code will help you and others to understand the code you write. Blocks of commented text within a SCRIPT tag can be preceded by "/*" and followed by "*/", as shown in Listing 2.1. Comments that fit on one line may be preceded with "//." The browser ignores commented text when the code is executed. Comments in HTML, however, use the more familiar HTML commenting characters ("<!-- html comments go here.-->").

The first line of the script begins with an HTML comment tag (<!--), which hides the script from older browsers (Netscape 1.0 and Internet Explorer 2 and earlier). If you neglect to include this tag in your scripts, these old browsers will display the text of your script in the body of the page.

The SCRIPT section contains four JavaScript statements. The first one uses the var keyword to initialize the new variable myTextContainer. Then the assignment operator (=) assigns the text "A Web browser " to the variable myTextContainer. In the next two lines the add-by-value operator (+=) adds additional text to the variable myTextContainer. Then the alert method of the window object displays the contents of the variable myTextContainer in a small alert box window. After the visitor clicks OK, the text in the BODY section of the HTML document is displayed.

Because you've studied HTML, you probably have a favorite text editor. Type the code from Listing 2.1 into your text editor, save the document as listing2.1.html, and open it in your favorite Web browser.

Script tag includes attributes for type and language

```
<html><head><title>alert me</title>
<script type="text/javascript" language="javascript">
<!--
//the var keyword initializes a variable.
var myTextContainer = "A web browser ";
myTextContainer += "will follow your instructions ";
myTextContainer += "exactly and without an argument.";
/*The alert method of the window object creates an
'alert box' that demands the attention of the visitor.*/
window.alert(myTextContainer);

// ends script hiding -->
</script>
</head>
<body bgcolor="white">
<p>Isn't it nice how computers do what they are
told?</p>
</body>
</html>
```

HTML comment code to hide the script from old browsers

JavaScript comment code hides the HTML comment code from the script

Listing 2.1 A Sequence of JavaScript Statements

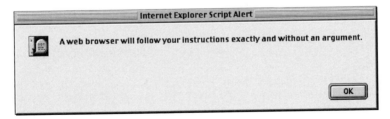

Internet Explorer Script Alert

A web browser will follow your instructions exactly and without an argument.

OK

Figure 2.1 The Output of Listing 2.1

๑๑ Looping: Doing Things Repeatedly

Have you ever noticed these instructions on a shampoo bottle?

"Lather, rinse, repeat."

If you were a computer, you would never leave the shower because these instructions create an endless loop. To avoid this problem, loop structures in JavaScript must be a bit more precise.

Perhaps the most common form of looping in JavaScript is the **for loop**. Here's the form:

```
for (initial expr. ; test condition ; update expr.){
   JavaScript statements go here.
}
```

The **initial expression** in a for loop consists of a variable set to an initial value. Programmers commonly use *i* as the **index variable** in for loops, but any variable name will do. Listing 2.2 assigns an initial value of 5 to the index variable i. A semicolon (;) separates the initial expression from the test condition.

The **test condition** determines when the loop ends. To avoid spending the rest of your life washing your hair, for example, you would modify the instructions on the shampoo bottle to read, "Lather, rinse, repeat. Stop when your hair is clean." In Listing 2.2, the test condition specifies that the loop should continue only while i is greater than one (i > 1). If i is one, the loop stops.

The **update expression** specifies how to change the index variable after each cycle of the loop finishes. In Listing 2.2, the **decrement operator** (--) reduces the value of i by 1 after each cycle of the loop.

Within the curly braces ({ }) are two statements. The first statement combines the current value of i with a text string and writes the result to the current Web document in the browser window. The second statement adds another sentence to the document. Notice that both statements contain the HTML break tag (<br>) as part of the text string. The <br> tag creates a line break. The loop then repeats until the value of i goes down to 1. When the loop ends, the JavaScript statements outside the curly braces then add two final lines of text to the document. Figure 2.2 shows the output of this example.

```
<html><head><title>loop me</title>
<script type="text/javascript" language="javascript">
<!--
for (i=5;i>1;i--){
   document.write(i + " bottles of root beer on the ¬
wall.<br>");
   document.write("You take one down, pour a round.<br>");
}
document.write("<br>There is only one bottle of root ¬
beer left.<br>");
```

```
document.write("<h1>Now stop drinking all my root ¬
beer.</h1>");
//-->
</script>
</head>
<body bgcolor="white">
</body>
</html>
```

Listing 2.2 The Classic For Loop in Action

Figure 2.2 Output of Listing 2.2

◎◎ Conditional Branching: Code That Makes Decisions

Web pages are more interesting when the content varies depending on the visitor's input. **Conditional branching** is the term that represents how a computer program follows different paths (branches) depending on circumstances. Conditional branching is usually implemented through if-else structures such as the one in Listing 2.3 (illustrated in Figure 2.3).

```
<html><head><title>prompt me</title>
<script type="text/javascript" language="javascript">
<!--

var yourSpecies = window.prompt("Are you human or ¬
alien?","");
if (yourSpecies == "human"){
   document.write("Greetings Earthling.<br>");
}else{
   document.write("Nanu nanu. Kaplagh!<br>");
}

//-->
</script>
</head>
<body bgcolor="white">
</body>
</html>
```

Listing 2.3 Conditional Branching with If-Else

In line 1 of the SCRIPT section, the prompt method of the window object asks the Web page visitor a question. The user types an answer, which is assigned to the variable yourSpecies.

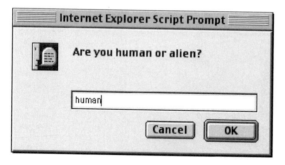

Figure 2.3 Asking a Question of the Web Page Visitor

Line 2 of Listing 2.3 tests the condition (yourSpecies == "human"). If the visitor typed human, the condition evaluates as true and "Greetings Earthling" is written to the current document. If the visitor types anything else, the condition evaluates as false and "Nanu nanu. Kaplagh!" is written to the current document.

☆ **WARNING Why Use ==?**

The most common error made by beginning programmers is to confuse the assignment operator (=) with the equality sign (==). In writing if-else structures, be sure to use the equality sign (==) to test your conditions. If you use the assignment operator by mistake, the condition you create will always evaluate as true and you won't get the results you desire.

◎◎ Placing Scripts in the HEAD Section

Web pages created with HTML are divided into two large sections. The HEAD section contains information about the page, such as the title and links to any style sheets. The BODY section contains the text, graphics, and media elements that will be visible to Web page visitors.

Scripts can be stored in both the HEAD and the BODY sections. The HEAD is used most often because it loads first. In this way, you can refer to your code in the BODY with the assurance that the code will be completely loaded into the browser's memory. Listing 2.4 shows a typical JavaScript-enhanced page with a script in the HEAD and a reference to that script in the BODY (see Figure 2.4).

In Listing 2.4, a value is **passed** (sent) from the onclick event handler in the BODY to the showText() function in the HEAD. The showText() function takes the value it receives and stores it in a temporary variable called inputdata. The alert method of the window object then displays the value found in inputdata as an alert window. The value being passed around is document.sampleform.userinfo.value, which represents the text the visitor typed into the userinfo field on the sampleform FORM of the current document.

```
<html>
<head><title>a place for scripts</title>
<script type="text/javascript" language="javascript">
<!--
function showText(inputdata){
  window.alert(inputdata);
}
//-->
</script>
</head>
<body bgcolor="white">
<p>Please type any text and then click the button.</p>
<form name="sampleform">
<input type="text" size=50 name="userinfo"><br><br>
<input type="button" name="mybutton" value="show text"
onclick="showText(document.sampleform.userinfo.value);">
</form>
</body>
</html>
```

> The onclick event handler sends the information typed by the visitor to the showText() function in the head. the showText() function then displays the information in an alert window.

Listing 2.4 Placing Scripts in the HEAD Section

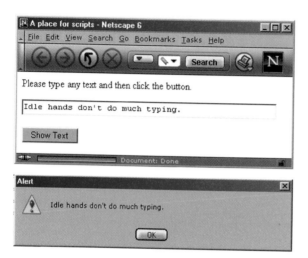

Figure 2.4 The Output of Listing 2.4

Creating Reusable Libraries of Your Favorite Code

In the long run, it's most efficient to store your favorite scripts in libraries. In that way, you won't have to retype functions every time you use them. For example, the function showText() from Listing 2.4 will likely be of use to you in other pages.

To create a library of your favorite code, create a plain text file in any text editor and then save the file with the extension .js. Listing 2.5 shows the complete contents of mylibrary.js. You will add more code to this library as you work through this book.

```
function showText(inputdata){
    window.alert(inputdata);
}
```

Listing 2.5 The Complete Contents of the File mylibrary.js

Listing 2.6 shows how easy it is to use your new library (see also Figure 2.5). You simply add the SRC attribute to the SCRIPT tag in the HEAD and then type the path to the library file. The HTML code creates two buttons. Both buttons call the showText() function stored in mylibrary.js, but the values they pass to the function differ.

```
<html><head><title>using external libraries of
code</title>
<script type="text/javascript" language="javascript"
src="mylibrary.js">
</script>
</head>
```

Code from the file 'mylibrary.js' is referenced here.

```
<body bgcolor="white">
<form name="sampleform">
<input type="button" value="Quote 1"
onclick="showText('If you want to have fun, then date ¬
a tenor.');">
<input type="button" value="Quote 2"
onclick="showText('If you want to be efficient, then ¬
database.');">
</form>
</body>
</html>
```

Listing 2.6 A Web page That Uses an External Code Library

☆ **WARNING**   **Single versus Double Quotes**

The `onclick` handler in Listing 2.6 contains both single and double quotes. The text in single quotes is **nested** within the text in double quotes. When you nest quotes in this way, the Web browser can correctly determine where each text expression begins and ends. As you debug your code, be sure to look for improperly nested quotes. It's a common error.

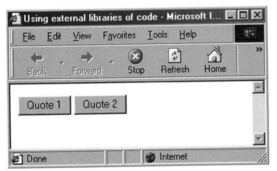

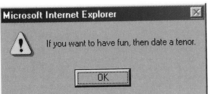

Figure 2.5 The Output of Listing 2.6

☆ **SHORTCUT**   **Debugging Your Scripts**

One of the easiest ways to detect errors in your code is to use the JavaScript **console** built into Netscape Communicator 4 or later. In Netscape 4, type **javascript:** and press Return in the location or netsite field of any Netscape window to bring up the JavaScript console. In Netscape 6, from the TASKS menu choose **TOOLS** and **JAVASCRIPT CONSOLE**. To view any errors generated by your code, keep the console open while you test your pages.

◎ Creating a Page to Make HTML Code

As you work through this book, you will create many Web pages containing all the standard HTML markup tags in addition to all the JavaScript code you will type. That is a lot of typing. With a little ingenuity, you can build a JavaScript-enhanced page to quickly create standard HTML code for use in your projects.

First, add the code in Listing 2.7 to your `mylibrary.js` file.

```
function buildPage(){
    var pagecontent = "<html><head><title>";
    pagecontent += document.pageform.pagetitle.value;
    pagecontent += "</title></head>\n";
    pagecontent += "<body bgcolor='white'>\n";
    pagecontent += document.pageform.bodytext.value;
    pagecontent += "\n</body>\n</html>";

    document.pageform.mycode.value=pagecontent;
}
```

Listing 2.7 The buildPage Function

Next, create a text file with the HTML code found in Listing 2.8.

```
<html><head><title>HTML Builder page</title>
<script type="text/javascript" language="javascript"
src="mylibrary.js">
</script>
</head>
<body bgcolor="white">
<h1>HTML Builder</h1>
<p>Fill out the form below to create a basic html
page.</p>
<form name="pageform">
<h2>Title:</h2>
<p>Type the title for your web page below.<br>
<input type="text" name="pagetitle" size="50" value="a
basic html page">
</p>
<h2>Body text:</h2>
<p>Type the body text for your page below.<br>
<textarea name="bodytext" cols="80" rows="10">
</textarea>
</p>
```

```
<p>
<input type="button" value="build my page"
onclick="buildPage();">
</p>
<h2>Code for you to copy will appear below.</h2>
<p>
<textarea name="mycode" cols="80" rows="15">
</textarea>
</p>
<p>Copy and paste the text into any text editor and save
it as an html file.</p>
</form>
</body>
</html>
```

Listing 2.8 The HTML Builder Web Page Code

☆TIP   View the completed HTML Builder page at http://www.awl.com/estrella/.

In Listing 2.8, notice the pageform HTML form containing three fields: pagetitle, bodytext, and mycode. Visitors will type text into the first two fields, click the button, and see HTML code displayed in the mycode field. This Web wizardry is possible because of the buildPage() function in the mylibrary.js file shown in Listing 2.7.

The buildPage() function begins by creating a variable called pagecontent. It then adds the standard HTML tags <html>, <head>, and <title>. After the <title> tag, the text from the pagetitle field is added to the variable pagecontent. Then the closing </title> and </head> tags are added. The **new line** code (/n) is then added to create a line break to aid readability. Next, the <body> tag is added. Then the text the visitor typed into the bodytext field is added. The closing </body> and </html> tags complete the code.

The final line of code places the complete contents of the variable pagecontent into the on-screen text field mycode. To be precise, the contents of the variable pagecontent are assigned to the value of the text field mycode of the form pageform of the current document (see Figure 2.6).

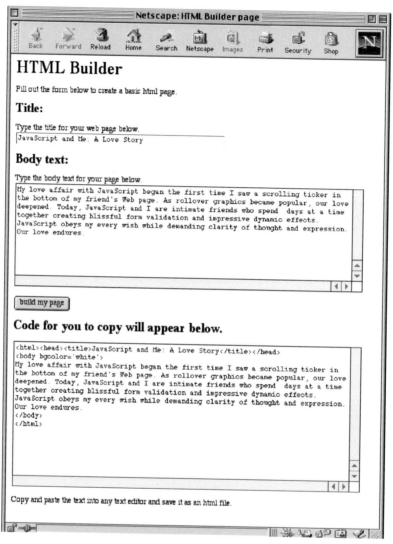

Figure 2.6 The Output of Listings 2.7 and 2.8

◎◎ Creating a Page to Test Code

Listing 2.9 creates a small page that may prove helpful to you as you work through the rest of this book. The page contains a form with a single field and a single button. The button calls the `runCode()` function, which in turn calls `eval()`, one of JavaScript's built-in functions. The `eval()` function takes whatever text is passed to it and attempts to execute the text as JavaScript code.

Use this page as you experiment with concepts and techniques throughout this book. For example, if you type `window.alert('some text');` into the field and then click the button, an alert window will appear displaying "some text."

```
<html><head><title>code testing page</title>
<script type='text/javascript' language='javascript'>
<!--
function runCode(){
   eval(document.codelab.codefield.value);
}
//-->
</script>
</head>
<body bgcolor='white'>
<h1>Experiment with JavaScript below</h1>
<form name="codelab">
<p><textarea name="codefield" rows=4 cols=60></textarea>
<br><br><input type="button" onclick="runCode();"
value="Run Code"></p>
</form>
</body>
</html>
```

Listing 2.9 A Page to Test Your JavaScript Code

Figure 2.7 shows the screen.

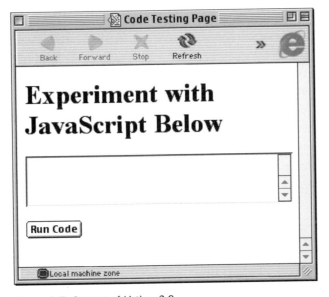

Figure 2.7 Output of Listing 2.9

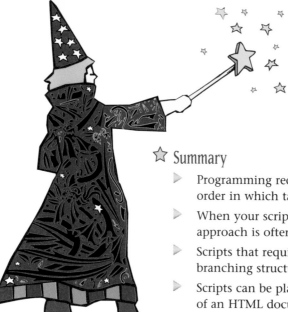

☆ Summary

▷ Programming requires an understanding of sequence, the order in which tasks are executed.

▷ When your script requires repetitive actions, the best approach is often a for loop.

▷ Scripts that require decision making use conditional branching structures such as if-else.

▷ Scripts can be placed in either the HEAD or BODY section of an HTML document but are usually placed in the HEAD.

▷ External libraries of often-used scripts make it easier to create multiple pages that share common functions.

▷ Using the eval() function makes it easy to create a script to test your JavaScript code.

☆ Online References

CNET.com's builder site on JavaScript basics.
```
http://builder.cnet.com/webbuilding/pages/Programming/
Javascript/ss01.html
```

☆ Review Questions

1. What is the assignment operator?

2. What is the add-by-value operator, and how is it useful?

3. What method of the window object is used to notify visitors of important information?

4. What are the four parts of a for loop structure?

5. Give an example of an if-else conditional branching structure.

6. What is the most common programming error made by beginners?

7. What is the advantage of placing scripts in the HEAD section?

8. How do you reference an external code library in the SCRIPT tag?

9. Why is it necessary to nest single and double quotes?

10. How is it possible to change the text of a text field in an HTML form?

☆ Hands-On Exercises

1. Create a set of five pages using the HTML Builder.

2. Set up the first page as the home page with links to all the other pages.

3. On the second page, demonstrate your understanding of sequence. Use Listing 2.1 as a model.

4. On the third page, demonstrate your understanding of looping. Use Listing 2.2 as a model.

5. On the fourth page, demonstrate your understanding of conditional branching. Use Listing 2.3 as a model.

6. On the fifth page, create a button that changes the value of a text field of an HTML form. Use Listing 2.8 as a model.

CHAPTER THREE

WORKING WITH FORMS

In Chapter Two you learned basic programming skills and concepts by manipulating the values found in FORM elements on a Web page. Much of this chapter focuses on manipulating the content of the VALUE property of HTML form elements such as text fields, selection menus, and radio buttons. Learning to control the content of HTML forms lets you gather information from your visitors, create on-line tests, and ensure that the values typed by your visitor are formatted appropriately before the form is sent to you.

Chapter Objectives

☆ To learn how to use form validation to examine the text entered by your visitors

☆ To understand the principles of working with text fields

☆ To learn how to detect and change the format of infor-mation in a text field

☆ To learn how to work with radio buttons, check boxes, and selection menus

☆ To create simple self-grading tests

◎ Form Validation

Imagine you're shopping at k9treats.com (not a real company). You've just clicked the button to add a box of liver treats to your online shopping cart. You then click the Check Out button. The next screen probably displays an HTML form that asks for your name, address, and credit card information. Suppose you type your name and address but neglect to type your credit card information. When you click Continue, text on the screen reminds you that you must enter a credit card number before proceeding.

The reminder screen was the result of a JavaScript technique known as **form validation**. When you clicked Continue, a JavaScript function was called. The function detected that there was no valid entry in the credit card field and created a page to remind you to enter the required information.

◎ Working with Text Fields

Text fields within a form are created with the HTML `<input type="text">` tag (for text input that fits on a single line) or the HTML `<textarea></textarea>` tag (for text input that requires multiple lines). You can assign names and values to both tags using the `NAME` and `VALUE` properties.

This means that when a visitor types something into a text field on your page, you can query the input field by name and find out the value the visitor typed. In many cases, you may wish to create a form with a required field. It is useful to be able to determine whether the visitor entered information into a required field before the form gets sent to you via e-mail. Listing 3.1 demonstrates a simple form validation procedure to make sure the visitor types something into the `visitor` text field before the form is mailed.

```
<html><head><title>Basic Form Validation</title>
<script type="text/javascript" language="JavaScript">
<!--
function validate(){
   if (!document.survey.visitor.value){
      alert("You must enter your name before submitting ¬
this form.");
      document.survey.visitor.focus();
      return false;
   }else{
      return true;
   }
}
```

```
//-->
</script>
</head>
<body bgcolor="white">
<h1>Visitor Color Preference Survey</h1>
<form action="mailto:jstext@stevenestrella.com"
method="POST" enctype="text/plain" name="survey"
onsubmit="return validate();">
```

> When the form is submitted, the `validate()` function is called. It returns a value of true or false. If true, then the information on the form is sent using the mailto method defined in the action attribute. If false, no mail is sent.

```
<p>Name (required): <input type="text" name="visitor"
value="" size="40"></p>

<p>Favorite Color: <input type="text" name="color"
value="" size="30"></p>

<p>What are your thoughts on using this survey?<br>
<textarea name="thoughts" rows="5" cols="50"
value=""></textarea></p>

<p><input type="submit" value="Send Survey"></p>
</form>
</body>
</html>
```

Listing 3.1 Simple Form Validation of a Text Field

How Does It Work?

The code in Listing 3.1 produces the following sequence of events.

1. The browser loads the HEAD section, which contains the JavaScript function `validate()`. That function is now in memory and ready to do its work when called.

2. The browser loads the BODY section and displays a level-1 heading <h1>.

3. A FORM object with the name `survey` begins to appear on the screen. The ACTION property is set to post the contents of the form, encoded as plain text, to an e-mail address.

4. Within the form, the `visitor` text input field appears with an instruction to the visitor to type a name. The `color` text input field appears with an instruction to the visitor to type a favorite color. The size properties of the two fields are set to different values because names of people are longer than the names of colors.

5. A TEXTAREA field is displayed that allows the user to type multiple lines of text to provide feedback on the survey.

6. An INPUT tag, of type submit, creates a Submit button. The value of Send Survey is the actual text displayed on the button.

7. Having typed nothing, the visitor clicks the Send Survey button to submit the form. The button generates a submit event.

8. The FORM object's onSubmit handler sends a line of code to the JavaScript interpreter in the browser. That line of code calls the validate() function and returns a value of true or false to the FORM object. If the value returned is false, the FORM object does not send the e-mail.

9. The validate() function begins with an if-else structure to check the value of the visitor field on the survey form. The code !document. survey.visitor.value might be translated to English as, "There is not a value in the visitor field of the survey form of the current document." In this case, that statement evaluates as true. An alert box appears with instructions. After the visitor dismisses the alert box, the pointer is placed conveniently on the visitor field using the focus() method. Finally, a value of false is returned to the FORM object that called the function, preventing the e-mail from being sent.

10. The visitor types a name in the visitor field and clicks the Send Survey button again. This time the validate() function detects a value in the required field and returns a value of true. The FORM object then sends its contents to the e-mail address listed in its ACTION property.

The form is shown in Figure 3.1.

The e-mail received from this form would consist of a series of name-value pairs:

```
visitor=Clara Belle Estrella
color=Yellow
thoughts=I came here for the liver treats and all I
found was this dumb form.
```

☆ **TIP   mailto: versus CGI**

The mailto: protocol (shown in Listing 3.1) will work on any Web browser that has been set up to send e-mail. Otherwise, it fails. The safest way to send e-mail from a form is to use a **Common Gateway Interface (CGI)** script running on your Web server. Most Web hosting services provide their clients with a standard CGI e-mail program that sends information entered on a form to a designated e-mail address. If you have an account where you may post your Web pages then you should ask your hosting service representative for instructions to use their CGI e-mail program. The mailto: alternative is suitable for our purposes, however, because it doesn't require an active Web hosting account.

Working with Text Fields

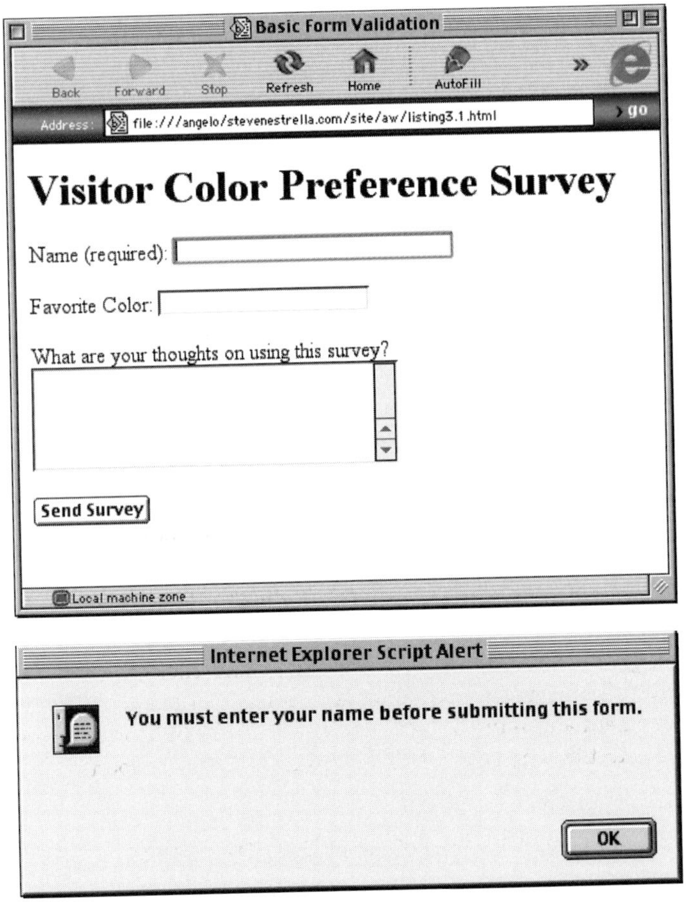

Figure 3.1 Output of Listing 3.1

Surveys often request e-mail addresses from Web page visitors. Because one wrong character in an e-mail address will render it invalid, it's important to encourage your visitors to type carefully. The briefest e-mail address possible would consist of a single character, the "@" symbol, another character, a dot ("."), and at least two characters for a domain name. An address such as Q@X.ca is unlikely but certainly possible. A validation function is needed to ensure that the @ symbol is present somewhere after the first character, the dot is present somewhere after the @ symbol with at least one character in between, and at least two characters follow the dot.

Listing 3.2 demonstrates how to validate an e-mail address and introduces the `indexOf()` method. Programmers use the `indexOf()` method to locate one or more characters in a text string. For example, if a variable called `myPet` has the value `Clara`, then `myPet.indexOf("C")` would yield the value 0 because the C is the first character in the string counting from zero. Similarly, `myPet.indexOf("a")` would yield the value 2 because a is character 2 when counting from zero. The location of the second a could be determined with `myPet.indexOf("a",3)`, which begins searching the text at character 3. In this case, `myPet.indexOf("a",3)` returns the value 4.

```html
<html><head><title>Email Address Form Validation</title>
<script type="text/javascript" language="JavaScript">
<!--
function validate(){
  var theEmail = document.survey.email.value;
  var atLoc = theEmail.indexOf("@",1);
  var dotLoc = theEmail.indexOf(".",atLoc+2);
  var len = theEmail.length;
  if (atLoc > 0 && dotLoc > 0 && len > dotLoc+2){
    return true;
  }else{
    alert("Please enter your e-mail address properly.");
    document.survey.email.focus();
    return false;
  }
}
//-->
</script>
</head>
<body bgcolor="white">
<h1>Visitor E-mail Survey</h1>

<form action="mailto:jstext@stevenestrella.com"
method="POST" enctype="text/plain" name="survey"
onsubmit="return validate();">
<p>E-mail Address (required): <input type="text"
name="email" value="" size="60"></p>

<p><input type="submit" value="Send Survey"></p>
</form>
</body>
</html>
```

> This expression returns true only if the @ symbol and a dot are present in the e-mail address and the length of the address is sufficient to include a two-character domain at the end.

Listing 3.2 E-mail Address Validation

How Does It Work?

Listing 3.2 produces the following sequence of events.

1. The browser loads the HEAD section, which contains the JavaScript function `validate()`. That function is now in memory and ready to do its work when called.

2. A FORM object named `survey` begins to appear on the screen. The ACTION property is set to post the contents of the form, encoded as plain text, to an e-mail address. Within the form, the text INPUT field `email` appears with an instruction to the visitor to type an e-mail address.

3. An INPUT tag of type `submit` creates a Submit button. The value of `Send Survey` is the text displayed on the button.

4. Having typed nothing, the visitor clicks the Send Survey button to submit the form. The button generates a `submit` event.

5. The `onsubmit` handler of the FORM object sends a line of code to the JavaScript interpreter in the browser. That code calls the `validate()` function and returns a value of `true` or `false` to the FORM object. If the value returned is `false`, the FORM object does not send the e-mail.

6. The `validate()` function creates a variable `theEmail` to hold the value typed by the visitor. A variable `atLoc` is created to hold the location of the @ character if it is character 1 or later (counting from zero). A variable `dotLoc` is created to hold the location of the "`.`" character if it is at least two characters after the @ symbol. A variable `len` is created to hold the length of the address typed by the visitor.

7. An if-else structure checks to see whether the location of @ is greater than 0, the location of "." is greater than 0, and the e-mail address ends at least two characters after the dot. The `&&` code is used to create the AND condition to check all three variables. If all of them are `true`, the `validate()` function returns `true` and the e-mail is sent. Otherwise, the visitor receives a polite alert.

◎◎ Changing Information in Text Fields

Sometimes the format of information received on a form must be specific. Phone numbers are one example. A standard U.S. telephone number such as (555) 333-4444 has a three-digit area code, a three-digit exchange, and a four-digit extension. The standard format uses parentheses to set off the area code and a hyphen between the exchange and the extension. Listing 3.3 demonstrates how the information typed in a text field can be reformatted automatically. You can apply this technique to Social Security numbers, ZIP codes, credit card numbers, or any number with a consistent structure.

```
<html><head><title>Automatic Field Formatting</title>
<script type="text/javascript" language="JavaScript">
<!--
function formatNumber(){
  var theNumbersOnly = "";
  var theChar = "";
  var theInput = document.phoneform.phone.value;

  for (i = 0; i < theInput.length; i++){
    theChar = theInput.substring(i,i+1);
    if (theChar >= "0" && theChar <= "9"){
      theNumbersOnly = "" + theNumbersOnly + theChar;
    }
  }

  if (theNumbersOnly.length < 10){
    alert("You must enter 10 numbers.");
    document.phoneform.phone.focus();
  }else{
    var areacode = theNumbersOnly.substring(0,3);
    var exchange = theNumbersOnly.substring(3,6);
    var extension = theNumbersOnly.substring(6,10);
    var newNumber = "(" + areacode + ") ";
    newNumber += exchange + "-" + extension;

    document.phoneform.phone.value = newNumber;
  }
}
//-->
</script>
</head>
<body bgcolor="WHITE">
<h1>Basic Automatic Formatting</h1>

<p>Type 10 numbers in any form and then press the tab
key.<br>
Your number will be formatted for the U.S. telephone
system.<br>
</p>

<form name="phoneform"><input type="text" name="phone"
value="(555) 555-1234" size="20"
onchange="formatNumber();"></form>
</body>
</html>
```

Listing 3.3 Automatic Field Formatting

Figure 3.2 shows the form.

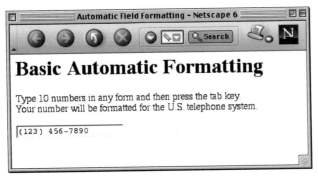

Figure 3.2 Output of Listing 3.3

How Does It Work?

Listing 3.3 generates the following sequence of events.

1. The browser loads the HEAD into memory and displays the BODY. Note that the text field `phone` has a value that will be displayed in the field when the page loads to help the visitor understand the format.

2. The visitor types numbers and other symbols into the text field.

3. The visitor presses ⎋Tab to move the cursor out of the field. Because the value of the field has changed, the browser receives a `change` event message.

4. The text field `phone` has a handler to respond to the change event. It calls the `formatNumber()` function defined in the HEAD.

5. The `formatNumber()` function creates a variable, `theNumbersOnly`, to hold numbers only. Any letters or other characters will be ignored.

6. A second variable, `theChar`, is created to hold each character while it is examined to determine whether it is a number.

7. A third variable, `theInput`, is created to hold the value the visitor typed.

8. A loop begins to examine each character in `theInput`. The loop begins at character 0 (the first character) and continues for the length of `theInput`. Each character is extracted from `theInput` using the `substring()` method. For example, `Steven.substring(0,3)` would return characters 0, 1, and 2 of the string `Steven`. In this case, the `substring()` method stops extracting characters when it reaches character 3. The result would be `Ste`.

9. A conditional structure examines the content of `theChar` to determine whether it lies within the range of 0 to 9. If `theChar` is a number, it is added to the variable `theNumbersOnly`. Notice that an empty text string (`" "`) is included in the math to make sure that `"123"` + `"456"` results in the text string `"123456"` rather than the number 579.

10. Another conditional structure then determines whether `theNumbersOnly` contains fewer than 10 characters. If it does, an alert box appears and the cursor is placed in the phone field.

11. If the number of characters in `theNumbersOnly` is 10 or more, variables are created to hold the area code, exchange, and extension portions of `theNumbersOnly`. Another variable, `newNumber`, is created to contain the properly formatted combination of the area code, exchange, and extension complete with parentheses and hyphen.

12. The value of the phone field is changed to `newNumber`. The visitor's number is reformatted to conform to U.S. telephone standards and is displayed on the screen.

◎◎ Working with Radio Buttons

Typical surveys contain questions to which only a limited number of answers make sense. A question on gender, for example, can be answered only "male" or "female." It makes little sense to use an open-ended text field in this case. Instead, you can use **radio buttons**, a series of buttons offering mutually exclusive selections. Listing 3.4 demonstrates how you can determine the value associated with a radio button your visitor clicks.

```
<html><head><title>Radio Button Form Validation</title>
<script type="text/javascript" language="JavaScript">
<!--
/* The getRadioValue function - store in mylibrary.js.*/
function getRadioValue(formname,radioname){
  var theRadioButtons = document[formname][radioname];
  for (i=0;i<theRadioButtons.length;i++){
    if (theRadioButtons[i].checked){
      return theRadioButtons[i].value;
    }
  }
}
/* The showRadioValue function - store in
mylibrary.js.*/
function showRadioValue(formname,radioname,thevalue){
  var theRadioButtons = document[formname][radioname];
  for (i=0;i<theRadioButtons.length;i++){
    var temp = theRadioButtons[i].value;
    if (temp == thevalue){
      theRadioButtons[i].checked = true;
    }
  }
}
```

```
function validate(){
  var chosenGender = getRadioValue("survey","gender");
  if (chosenGender==null){
    alert("Is this a tough question?");
    return false;
  }
  if (chosenGender == "male"){
    document.survey.feedback.value = "Thank you sir.";
  }else{
    document.survey.feedback.value = "Thank you ¬
madame.";
  }
  return true;
}
function changeGender(){
  if (getRadioValue("survey","gender")==null){
    document.survey.feedback.value = "Gender not ¬
specified.";
    return;
  }
  if (getRadioValue("survey","gender")=="male"){
    showRadioValue('survey','gender','female');
    document.survey.feedback.value = "Thank you ¬
madame.";
  }else{
    showRadioValue('survey','gender','male');
    document.survey.feedback.value = "Thank you sir.";
    return;
  }
}
//-->
</script>
</head>
<body bgcolor="white">
<h1>Visitor Gender Survey</h1>
<form action="mailto:jsradio@stevenestrella.com"
method="POST" enctype="text/plain" name="survey"
onsubmit="return validate();">
<p>Name:<input type="text" name="visitor" value=""
size="40"></p>

<p>Gender:<input type="radio" name="gender"
value="male">Male
<input type="radio" name="gender"
value="female">Female</p>
```

```
<p><input type="button" value="Change Gender" onclick=
"changeGender();"></p>

<p><input type="submit" value="Send Survey"></p>

<hr>
<p>Feedback:<br>
<input type="text" name="feedback" value=""
size="50"></p>
</form>
</body>
</html>
```

Listing 3.4 Radio Button Form Validation

☆**SHORTCUT   Put It in the Library**

The getRadioValue() and showRadioValue() functions from listing 3.4 control the value checked on a set of radio buttons in a FORM. You will create many pages with radio buttons—including examples later in this book—so it makes sense to store these functions in mylibrary.js rather than copy them into every page.

How Does It Work?

Listing 3.4 generates the following sequence of events.

1. The browser loads the HEAD into memory and displays the BODY.

2. The BODY contains a FORM object named survey and an array of two radio button objects named gender. When multiple radio buttons share the same name, the browser creates an array in memory to hold the related radio buttons. The individual radio buttons in the array are assigned to elements in the new array. In this case, gender[0] is the radio button for male, and gender[1] is the one for female. Neither radio button is checked by default.

3. The visitor clicks the Send Survey button to submit the form. The button generates a submit event.

4. The FORM object's onsubmit handler sends a line of code to the JavaScript interpreter in the browser. This code calls the validate() function and returns a value of true or false to the FORM object. If the value returned is false, the FORM object does not send the e-mail.

5. The validate() function begins by creating a variable called chosenGender and setting its initial value to the value returned by the getRadioValue() function. The getRadioValue() function receives two parameters: the name of the form and the name of the radio button set.

> **☆ TIP   Pass Me That Value**
>
> You probably first encountered the term "parameter" in your high school algebra class. A parameter is a container for values. You can think of a parameter as a type of variable. In JavaScript the term "parameter" refers to any variable required for a function to do its job. A function to convert Farenheit to Celsius, for example, would require a parameter to hold the Fahrenheit temperature value. The expression convertToCelsius(temperature) calls the conversion function and passes the value found in the temperature parameter.

The `document` object contains an array of all its subsidiary objects, including the `FORM` called `survey`. The `FORM survey` in turn creates an array of all its subsidiary objects, including the radio button set `gender`. The expression `document["survey"]["gender"]` can then be used to identify the radio button set. The entire radio button set is an object that is then stored in the new variable `theRadioButtons`, which is itself an array consisting of two buttons: one for male and one for female. A loop then proceeds through each element of `theRadioButtons` to determine whether any of them is checked. If it finds that a radio button is checked, it returns the value of that radio button (`male` or `female`) to the `validate()` function, which places that value into `chosenGender`. If no radio button is checked, the value of `chosenGender` will be `null`, meaning that it is empty. Note that `null` is not in quotes because it is not a text string. Instead, it indicates the absence of any value.

6. The next section of the code contains three conditional structures to check for the three possible values that might be in `chosenGender`: `null`, `male`, or `female`.

7. If neither radio button is checked, it means that `chosenGender` is empty. An alert box appears with instructions. After the visitor dismisses the alert box, a value of `false` is returned to the `FORM` object that called the function, and that prevents the e-mail from being sent. The script ends as soon as a value is returned, so `chosenGender` is not tested further. If `chosenGender` contains any other value, the script continues.

8. If `chosenGender` is `male`, the text `Thank you sir` is placed into the `feedback` field located directly below the Send Survey button.

9. If `chosenGender` is `female`, the text `Thank you madame` is placed into the `feedback` field.

10. A value of `true` is returned to the `FORM` object, which then sends the form contents via e-mail to the address listed in the `ACTION` property.

11. Rarely, a visitor may wish to change the response to the gender question. For that reason, a button is provided labeled Change Gender. It calls the `changeGender()` function when clicked. The `changeGender()` function calls the `getRadioValue()` function to determine which radio button is checked. If none is checked, `Gender not specified` is displayed in the `feedback` field. Otherwise, the `showRadioValue()` function is called to change the checked radio button to the opposite gender.

12. The `showRadioValue()` function receives three parameters: the name of the FORM, the name of the radio button set, and the value of the radio button to be checked. A variable `theRadioButtons` is again created to hold the array of radio buttons. A loop steps through each element of the `theRadioButton` array to determine whether its value matches the desired value. If it does, the checked property of that radio button is set to `true`, and that causes the button to appear checked. Control returns to the `changeGender()`, function which displays `Thank you madame` or `Thank you sir` as appropriate (see Figure 3.3).

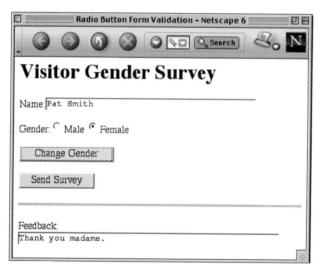

Figure 3.3 Output of Listing 3.4

Working with Check Boxes

Survey questions often employ **check boxes** to allow visitors to "check all that apply." Each check box can be assigned name and value properties. Each check box exists in either an unchecked or a checked state. When a form is submitted, the names and values of any checked boxes are sent with the form. The names and values of the unchecked boxes are not sent. To determine which boxes are checked, you test for the checked property. Listing 3.5 demonstrates the use of check boxes in a simple survey of education levels.

```
<html><head><title>Check Box Form Validation</title>
<script type="text/javascript" language="JavaScript">
<!--
function validate(){
  var degree = "";
  var comments = new Array(4);
  comments [0] = 'You are competent.';
  comments [1] = 'You are educated.';
  comments [2] = 'You are highly educated.';
  comments [3] = 'You spent too much time in school.';

  for (i=0;i< 4;i++){
    if (document.survey['degree'+i].checked){
      degree = document.survey['degree'+i].value;
      document.survey.feedback.value = comments[i];
    }
  }
```

The survey form has html checkboxes called degree1, degree2, etc. By adding the current value of i to the word degree, this conditional structure checks to see if a particular box is checked.

```
  if (degree == ""){
    alert("You need to get an education!");
    return false;
  }else{
    return true;
  }
}
//-->
</script>
</head>
<body bgcolor="white">
<h1>Visitor Education Survey</h1>

<form action="mailto:jscheckbox@stevenestrella.com"
method="POST" enctype="text/plain" name="survey"
onsubmit="return validate();">
<p>Name:<input type="text" name="visitor" value=""
size="40"></p>

<h4>Degrees you have earned (check all that apply):</h4>

<input type="checkbox" name="degree0" value="H.S.">
High School Diploma<br>
<input type="checkbox" name="degree1" value="B.A.">
Bachelor's Degree<br>
<input type="checkbox" name="degree2" value="M.A.">
Master's Degree<br>
```

```
<input type="checkbox" name="degree3" value="Ph.D.">
Doctorate<br>
<p><input type="submit" value="Send Survey"></p>

<hr>
<p>Feedback:<br>
<input type="text" name="feedback" value="" size="50">
</p>
</form>
</body>
</html>
```

Listing 3.5 Check Box Form Validation

Figure 3.4 shows the form.

Figure 3.4 Output of Listing 3.5

☆ **SHORTCUT**   **What's in a Name?**

When you create surveys or tests, it usually makes sense to name the text fields, radio buttons, or check boxes with sequential names such as "q1," "q2," "q3," and so on. Using a consistent and sequential naming scheme allows you to use a loop efficiently to poll the values in these form elements.

How Does It Work?

Listing 3.5 generates the following sequence of events.

1. The browser loads the `HEAD` into memory and displays the `BODY`.

2. The `BODY` contains a `FORM` object named `survey`. `FORM` objects automatically create an array of all form elements enclosed by the `<form>` and `</form>` tags. The names of the four check boxes in this form are `degree` followed by a number from 0 to 3. The number can be stored in a variable. In this way, you can use an expression such as `document.survey['degree'+x].checked` to determine whether a given box is checked. None of the boxes here is checked by default.

3. The visitor clicks the Send Survey button to submit the form, and the button generates a `submit` event. The `FORM` object handles the event by calling the `validate()` function. If `validate()` returns `true`, the form content is sent by e-mail.

4. The `validate()` function begins by creating a variable called `degree` and setting its initial value to an empty text string. Then an array is created to hold the four comments associated with the four degrees.

5. The `validate()` function loops through a series of statements four times while an index variable (`i`) counts from 0 to 3. On each pass through the loop, an element of the form survey is examined to see whether it is checked. That element is determined by combining `degree` with the current value of the index variable (`i`).

6. If a checked box is found, its value is stored in the `degree` variable. If multiple degrees are checked, each one will replace the previous contents of the `degree` variable.

7. The index variable of this loop (`i`) is used to determine which element of the comments array should be displayed in the feedback field.

8. The next section of the code contains conditional structures to test the value of the `degree` variable.

9. If none of the boxes is checked, it means that `degree` is empty. An alert box appears with instructions. After the visitor dismisses the alert box, a value of `false` is returned to the `FORM` object that called the function, and that prevents the e-mail from being sent.

10. If `degree` contains anything other than an empty text string, a value of `true` is returned to the `FORM` object, which then sends the form contents via e-mail to the address listed in the `ACTION` property.

11. The recipient receives an e-mail message containing a name-value pair for each checkbox.

◎◎ Working with Selection Menus

Another convenient way to present multiple options on a survey question is to use **selection menus**. The `<select>` tag creates a pop-up selection menu on the screen with the menu items as indicated in the `<option>` tags. Listing 3.6 demonstrates how to determine the value of the command selected by your visitor. In this example (see Figure 3.5), the visitor chooses a favorite Web site and can click a button to view it in a new window. After making a selection, the visitor can submit the form by e-mail. This **select and go navigation** is an increasingly popular use of selection menus.

```
<html><head><title>Selection Menu Form Validation</title>
<script type="text/javascript" language="JavaScript">
<!--
var chosenSite = "";
```
> `chosenSite` is a global variable because it is declared outside any function. The value in `chosenSite` will be available to all functions on the page.

```
/* The getSelectValue function - store in
mylibrary.js.*/
function getSelectValue(formname,selectname){
   var theMenu = document[formname][selectname];
   var selecteditem = theMenu.selectedIndex;
   return theMenu.options[selecteditem].value;
}
/* The showSelectValue function - store in
mylibrary.js.*/
function showSelectValue(formname,selectname,thevalue){
   var theMenu = document[formname][selectname];
   for (i=0;i<theMenu.options.length;i++){
     var temp = theMenu.options[i].value;
     if (temp == thevalue){
        theMenu.selectedIndex = i;
     }
   }
}
function validate(){
   chosenSite = getSelectValue("survey","websites");
   if (chosenSite == ""){
     alert("Please select your favorite Web site.");
     return false;
   }else{
     return true;
   }
}
function openSite(){
   chosenSite = getSelectValue("survey","websites");
   if (chosenSite == ""){
```

```
      alert("Please select your favorite Web site.");
    }else{
      window.location.href = chosenSite;
  }
}
//-->
</script>
</head>
<body bgcolor="white">
<h1>Visitor Site Preference Survey</h1>

<form action="mailto:jsselect@stevenestrella.com"
method="POST" enctype="text/plain" name="survey"
onsubmit="return validate();">
<p>Name:<input type="text" name="visitor" value=""
size="40"></p>

<h4>Choose your favorite Web site:</h4>

<select name="websites">
<option selected>Select a site</option>
<option value="http://www.javascript.com/">javascript.com
</option>
<option value="http://www.beatnik.com/">
beatnik.com</option>
<option value="http://www.awl.com/">Addison-
Wesley</option>
<option value="http://www.stevenestrella.com/">
The Author's Web Site</option>
</select>

<p><input type="button" value="Show Author's Choice"
onclick="showSelectValue('survey','websites', ¬
'http://www.beatnik.com/');"></p>

<input type="button" value="Go There!"
onclick="openSite();">

<p><input type="submit" value="Send Survey"></p>
</form>
</body>
</html>
```

Listing 3.6 Selection Menu Form Validation with Navigation Button

☆ **SHORTCUT   Put It in the Library**

Be sure to add the `getSelectValue()` and `showSelectValue()` functions from listing 3.6 to your `mylibrary.js` file. These functions control the value chosen on a SELECT menu in a FORM. Since you will create many pages with SELECT menus, it makes sense to store these functions in `mylibrary.js` rather than copy them into every page.

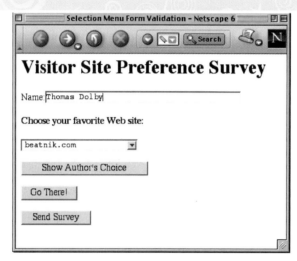

Figure 3.5 Output of Listing 3.6

How Does It Work?

Listing 3.6 generates the following sequence of events.

1. The browser loads the page and creates the necessary **FORM** and **SELECT** objects in memory. A global variable called **chosenSite** is created with an initial value of an empty text string. The three functions in the **HEAD** will use this variable, so it must be placed outside any of the functions.

2. The visitor chooses a command from the **SELECT** menu labeled "Select a site" and then clicks the Go There! button. That button is an input of type "button" with an **onclick** handler that calls the **openSite()** function.

3. The **openSite()** function, in the **HEAD**, calls the **getSelectValue()** function and passes the name of the form (**survey**) and the name of the select menu (**websites**) to determine the visitor's choice.

4. The **getSelectValue()** function creates a temporary variable called **theMenu** and fills it with the **websites SELECT** object on the **survey** form. It does this by exploiting the built-in arrays of the **document** and **form** objects. The **document** contains an array of all objects on the page.

The `FORM survey` is one such object. The expression `document["sur-vey"]` then represents the `FORM`. In turn, the form creates another array of all its objects. The `SELECT websites` is one such object. The expression `document["survey"]["websites"]` then represents the `SELECT` object called `websites`. Because `survey` and `websites` are stored in variables, the expression `document[formname][selectname]` properly references the `SELECT` object called `websites`.

A second variable, `selectedItem`, is then filled with the `selectedIndex` of `theMenu`. The `selectedIndex` refers to the number of the chosen command on the `SELECT` menu. The numbering begins with 0. The value of the chosen command on `theMenu` can then be determined with the expression `theMenu.options[selecteditem].value`. This works because the `SELECT` object contains an array of its `OPTIONS`. In this case, option number 1 (the second option when numbered from 0) is `javascript.com` with a value of `http://www.javascript.com`. The expression `document.survey.websites.options[1].value` would return the value `http://www.javascript.com`. Because the first part of that expression is assigned to the variable `theMenu`, it is possible to use the expression `theMenu.options[1].value` instead.

5. The global variable `chosenSite` now contains the value of the command chosen by the visitor. The `getSelectValue()` function is finished with its work, so the `openSite()` function continues to the next line.

6. The variable `chosenSite` is tested to see whether it is empty. If it is, the visitor receives an alert box with instructions to select something.

7. If the visitor has selected something, the browser loads the site chosen by the visitor. The code `window.location.href = URL` loads the given URL into the `href` property of the `location` object of the current `window`. Because the `location` object stores the URL of the currently loaded document in its `HREF` property, changing the value of the `HREF` property causes the browser to load the new page.

8. The visitor becomes overwhelmed with curiosity about which site is preferred by the author of the page. The visitor clicks the button labeled Show Author's Choice, which calls the `showSelectValue()` function and passes three parameters: the name of the `FORM` (`survey`), the name of the `SELECT` (`websites`), and the value to display (`http://www.beatnik.com`).

9. The `showSelectValue()` function steps through the elements of the array of options in the `SELECT` until it finds a value that matches the desired value. Then it sets the `selectedIndex` of the `SELECT` to the number of the option with the matching value. The displayed text of the `SELECT` changes to match the new value.

☆ WARNING **Global Versus Local Variables**

When you create a variable within a function, the variable is local to the function. This means that other functions in the script will not understand any references to the local variable. If a variable must be shared among functions, be sure to declare it outside any particular function, as shown in Listing 3.6 with the global variable chosenSite.

◎◎ Creating a Self-Grading Test

Educators often use forms to create self-grading diagnostic tests for students to use on the Web. Sometimes the content of the form is not submitted; instead, feedback is presented to the student to aid in studying the content. Listing 3.7 presents a simple, three-question test on music history.

```html
<html><head><title>Selection Menu Diagnostic Quiz</title>
<script type="text/javascript" language="JAVASCRIPT" src=
"mylibrary.js">
</script>

<script type="text/javascript" language="JavaScript">
<!--
var correctAnswers = new Array();
correctAnswers[1] = "1750";
correctAnswers[2] = "1791";
correctAnswers[3] = "1827";

function checkAnswers(){
  var score = 0;
  for (i=1; i<4; i++){
    deathDate = getSelectValue("quiz","q" + i);
    if (deathDate == correctAnswers[i]){
      score++;
    }
  }
  document.quiz.scorefield.value = score;
}
//-->
</script>
</head>
<body bgcolor="white">
<h1>Diagnostic Quiz on Composer Dates</h1>

<form name="quiz">
<h4>Question 1: What is Bach's year of death?</h4>
```

```
<select name="q1">
<option selected>Select your answer</option>
<option value="1670">1670</option>
<option value="1685">1685</option>
<option value="1695">1695</option>
<option value="1725">1725</option>
<option value="1750">1750</option>
</select>

<h4>Question 2: What is Mozart's year of death?</h4>

<select name="q2">
<option selected>Select your answer</option>
<option value="1750">1750</option>
<option value="1765">1765</option>
<option value="1773">1773</option>
<option value="1791">1791</option>
<option value="1812">1812</option>
</select>

<h4>Question 3: What is Beethoven's year of death?</h4>

<select name="q3">
<option selected>Select your answer</option>
<option value="1770">1770</option>
<option value="1791">1791</option>
<option value="1827">1827</option>
<option value="1833">1833</option>
<option value="1841">1841</option>
</select>

<hr>
<p><input type="button" value="Check Answers" onclick=
"checkAnswers();"></p>

<p>Your score is:<input type="text" name="scorefield"
value="" size="10"></p>
</form>
</body>
</html>
```

Listing 3.7 Quiz with Selection Menus

Figure 3.6 shows the form.

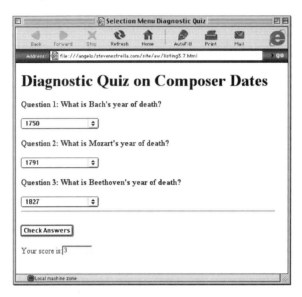

Figure 3.6 Output of Listing 3.7

☆ **WARNING** No Peeking!

A visitor to the page created by Listing 3.7 could cheat by viewing the source code. To avoid this problem, you can hide the answers by placing the script section in an external library. Be aware, however, that experienced computer users can locate the text of the external library. With that in mind, such online tests are suitable as diagnostic study aids but should not be used to determine grades.

How Does It Work?

Listing 3.7 generates the following sequence of events.

1. The browser loads the HEAD section of the page into memory. This includes an array containing the correct answers to the quiz. Element 0 of the array is not filled with any value; as a result, the element numbers begin with 1 to match the question numbers.

2. The BODY portion of the page is loaded. The SELECT objects on the page are created and given sequential names "q1", "q2", and "q3".

3. The visitor selects answers to each of the questions and clicks the Check Answers button. The onclick handler calls the checkAnswers() function.

4. The checkAnswers() function creates a variable called score and sets it to 0.

5. The checkAnswers() function performs a loop. On each pass through the loop, an index variable (i) increases in value by 1 until it reaches 4.

6. The checkAnswers() function creates a temporary variable called theMenu and fills it with the SELECT object on the survey form having the name q1, q2, or q3 depending on the value of i. A second variable, selectedItem, is then filled with the selectedIndex of theMenu.

7. A temporary variable called deathDate is created and filled with the value of the selected option of theMenu.

8. The index variable of this loop (i) is then used to determine which element of the correctAnswers array is to be compared to the value of deathDate. If the values match, the score variable increases by 1. The operator ++ is an abbreviation used to increment a variable by 1.

9. Finally, the score is assigned to the value of the scorefield text input on the quiz form. The visitor's score appears in the text field on the screen.

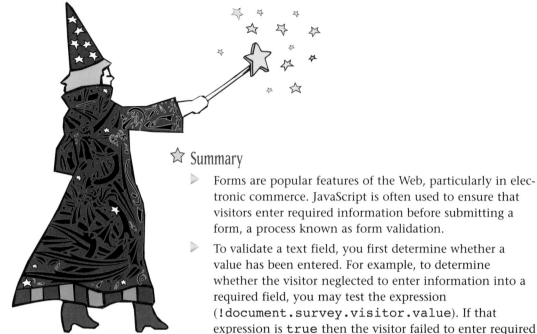

☆ Summary

▷ Forms are popular features of the Web, particularly in electronic commerce. JavaScript is often used to ensure that visitors enter required information before submitting a form, a process known as form validation.

▷ To validate a text field, you first determine whether a value has been entered. For example, to determine whether the visitor neglected to enter information into a required field, you may test the expression (`!document.survey.visitor.value`). If that expression is `true` then the visitor failed to enter required information into the visitor field. You can also check to make sure the information is in the correct format in terms of numbers and punctuation.

▷ You can create JavaScript code that will change the format of visitor-entered text if it is in the wrong format for your purposes.

▷ Browsers automatically store a set of radio buttons, all bearing the same name, in an array. For example, if you have two radio buttons called gender, the first one, `gender[0]`, might have a value of `male` and the second one, `gender[1]`, might have a value of `female`. You can use JavaScript expressions to see which button is checked and to find its value.

▷ Often, it makes sense to create a series of check boxes with sequential names such as `degree1`, `degree2`, and so on. You can then use a loop to determine which ones are checked.

▷ A common technique for obtaining the value of a selected item in a `SELECT` menu is to store the `SELECT` object in a variable, find the number of the selected option (the `selectedIndex` property), and then find the value of the selected option.

▷ A variant of form validation allows you to create self-grading online study aids.

☆ Online References

Dr. Estrella's Interactive Web Programming. This site contains examples of form validation. Look in the "Scripts to Study" section for examples.
`http://www.stevenestrella.com/IWP`

W3Schools.com has a collection of useful form validation examples.
`http://www.w3schools.com/js/js_form.asp`

☆ Review Questions

1. How is the `focus()` method used in form validation?

2. When the visitor clicks the Submit button on a form, how does the Web browser know what to do next?

3. What method is used to extract one or more characters from a string of text?

4. A visitor changes a value in a text field and presses the ⟨Tab⟩ key. What event handler is needed to respond to this action?

5. What property of an array can be used to find out the number of elements in the array?

6. How can you test to see whether a radio button is checked? How can you obtain the value of a radio button?

7. If you wish to use a loop to find the values of a series of check boxes, what scheme should you use to name the check boxes?

8. What happens when a validation function returns false?

9. What is the `selectedIndex` property?

10. What is a global variable? What is a local variable?

☆ Hands-On Exercises

1. Create a five-question, self-grading study aid using text fields for the responses.

2. Create a five-question, self-grading study aid using radio buttons for the responses.

3. Create a five-question, self-grading study aid using check boxes for the responses.

4. Create a five-question, self-grading study aid using selection menus for the responses.

5. Add form validation and a mailto action to each of the previous exercises. Use form validation to make sure that the visitor enters a name, and have the contents of the form sent to your e-mail address.

CHAPTER FOUR

IMAGE SWAPPING

In Chapter One you learned a basic technique, called a rollover, for replacing an image on a Web page after the page has already loaded. That technique works but has some disadvantages. The greatest drawback is that the second image takes a few seconds to appear on the screen when the mouse is rolled over the first image. A slow Internet connection would magnify this delay. A better technique is to download all your graphics to the visitor's hard drive before any rollovers occur. In that way, the second image in a rollover graphic appears very quickly because the visitor's browser has the image stored in its cache folder.

Chapter Objectives

☆ To learn how to code a simple rollover
☆ To find out how to preload image files into the browser's cache folder.

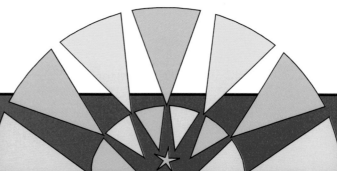

☆ To learn how to create a navigation page with multiple rollover images

☆ To understand how to create a double-rollover page

◎◎ Creating a Simple Rollover

Let's begin with a simple example. Figure 4.1 shows two image files created with the text tool in a graphics program. The image on the left depicts the word *Beethoven* in a stylized typeface with a nice drop-shadow effect. The image on the right is exactly the same size and adds a glow effect.

Figure 4.1 Two Versions of a Simple Image

Listing 4.1 creates a simple page to display the first image. Note that the SRC property of the IMG tag indicates that the image file beethovenoff.jpg resides in a folder called images located in the same folder as the HTML file itself.

Also note that the name property is set to beethoven. When the Web browser loads this page, an image object called beethoven will exist in the browser's memory. This object can be referenced in JavaScript as either document.beethoven or document['beethoven'].

☆ **SHORTCUT**   The form document['beethoven'] is much more useful because it refers to the 'beethoven' object as one in an array of objects belonging to the current document. It also gives you the flexibility to refer to the image name as an expression or variable rather than having to literally type beethoven each time.

```
<html><head><title>Rollover Beethoven</title></head>
<body bgcolor="white">
<div align="center">
<h1>Rollover Beethoven</h1>
<img src="images/beethovenoff.jpg" width="250"
height="70" name="beethoven" border="0"
alt="Picture of Beethoven">
</div>
</body>
</html>
```

It is good form to include the alt tag. This tag provides content for those browsing the Web with images turned off.

Listing 4.1 HTML Page Displaying a Single Image

To create a crude rollover effect, the SRC property of the 'beethoven' image must be changed to another image file only when the mouse is moved over the image. Unfortunately, the image objects created by most browsers do not respond to mouse events. The link objects created by the anchor tags (`<a></a>`), however, do respond to mouse events. By surrounding the IMG tag with a simple link, you can work around the limitations of current browsers (see Listing 4.2).

```
<html><head><title>Rollover Beethoven</title></head>
<body bgcolor="white">
<div align="center">
<h1>Rollover Beethoven</h1>
<a href="#" onmouseover=
"document['beethoven'].src='images/beethovenon.jpg';"
onmouseout=
"document['beethoven'].src='images/beethovenoff.jpg';">
<img src="images/beethovenoff.jpg" width="250"
height="70" name="beethoven"
border="0" alt="Picture of Beethoven"></a>
</div>
</body>
</html>
```

> The Anchor tag responds to mouseover and mouseout events.

> border="0" prevents the border of the image from appearing in the same color as the other links on the page.

Listing 4.2 The IMG Tag Surrounded by a Link with Mouse Event Handlers

How Does It Work?

Listing 4.2 produces the following sequence of events.

1. An IMG tag in the HTML code causes an image to appear in the current document displayed in a Web browser window.

   a. The name property in the IMG tag creates an image object in the browser's memory called beethoven with the height and width as specified.

   b. The SRC property of the IMG tag assigns the image file beethovenoff.jpg to the SRC property of the image object beethoven. The image then appears on the screen.

   c. The BORDER property is set to 0 to prevent the link color from showing around the borders of the image.

   d. The HREF property is set to a null value (#) so that no page is loaded if the visitor clicks on the graphic. If desired, this value can be changed to point to any Web page.

2. The visitor moves the mouse on top of the image. A mouseover event is generated in the browser's memory. The anchor tag handles the mouseover event by sending a single line of JavaScript code to the browser. That line of code instructs the browser to find the image beethovenon.jpg located in a folder called images in the same location as the current document. Depending on the size of the image and the speed of the connection, retrieving the image may take seconds or minutes.

3. The browser loads `beethovenon.jpg` into its memory and assigns it to replace the image file currently assigned to the SRC property of the image object `beethoven` loaded in the current `document`.

4. The browser displays the new image file in the same location as the old one. The image swap on rollover is accomplished.

◎◎ Creating a More Effective Rollover by Preloading Images

The technique just described is simple and easy to understand. Unfortunately, it produces an unacceptable delay in retrieving and displaying the second image. Listing 4.3 corrects the problem by preloading the image files. Read the comments in the code carefully to understand how it works.

```
<html><head><title>Rollover Beethoven</title>
<script type='text/javascript' language='Javascript'>
<!--
var theOffImage = new Image;
var theOnImage = new Image;

theOffImage.src = "images/beethovenoff.jpg";
theOnImage.src = "images/beethovenon.jpg";

function rollOn(imagename){
   document[imagename].src = theOnImage.src;
}
/*A similar function to handle the mouseout events*/
function rollOff(imagename){
   document[imagename].src = theOffImage.src;
}
//-->
</script>
</head>
<body bgcolor="white">
<div align="center">
<h1>Rollover Beethoven</h1>
<a href="#" onmouseover="rollOn('beethoven');"
onmouseout="rollOff('beethoven');"><img
src="images/beethovenoff.jpg"
width="250" height="70" name="beethoven" border="0"
alt="Picture of Beethoven"></a>
</div>
</body>
</html>
```

> Creates blank image objects in the browser's memory and assigns them to the variable names listed here.

> Fills the SRC properties of the new images with graphic files. Because all the code in the HEAD part of a web page loads before the body, all the image files listed here will begin loading before anything appears on the screen.

> A function to handle the mouseover events. Because the images are preloaded, the image swap will happen very quickly when this function is called.

Listing 4.3 New and Improved Rollover Technique

How Does It Work?

Listing 4.3 produces the following sequence of events.

1. The browser loads the HEAD portion of the HTML document into its memory.

2. The browser creates two blank image objects called theOffImage and theOnImage.

3. The browser fills the SRC properties of the new images by retrieving graphics files found in the images folder, which is located in the same folder as the current document. The image files are now located in the browser's cache folder on the visitor's hard drive.

4. The browser loads the rollOn() and rollOff() functions into memory. These functions do nothing until they are called.

5. The browser loads the BODY section of the document. An IMG tag in the HTML code causes an image to appear in the current document, and the browser creates an image object called beethoven as one of an array of objects in its internal map of the document.

6. The visitor moves the mouse on top of the image. A mouseover event is generated in the browser's memory.

7. The anchor tag handles the mouseover event by calling the function rollOn() and passing the name of the image, beethoven, to the function.

8. The rollOn() function takes the name of the image beethoven and puts it into a variable called imagename. It then finds the value of the SRC property of the image object theOnImage (from step 3) and assigns it to replace the SRC property of the beethoven image object. The image swap on rollover is accomplished.

9. The visitor moves the mouse outside the image, and the function rollOff() swaps the image back to the original.

This technique is more complex but much more effective because there is no image swap delay. The technique is also flexible enough to be used with multiple image rollovers on a single page.

☆**WARNING** Take some extra time to study the steps and concepts in Listing 4.3 before proceeding. When you're learning to program, diligence at the beginning pays off in less time spent debugging code later.

☆**TIP   Dealing with Old Browsers**

A few Web visitors use browsers that do not recognize the Image object as a part of their document object models. To avoid generating errors when your page loads in these early browsers, you may wish to include a conditional statement to test for the presence of the document.images array. This array exists only in the memory of browsers that support the Image object. The next examples show how to implement this safeguard.

⊚⊚ Creating Multiple Rollover Images

Listing 4.4 creates a single Web page with four images, each of which displays a glowing image on rollover. Notice that the `rollOn()` and `rollOff()` functions have been replaced with a single `swapImage()` function.

```
<html><head><title>Rollover Composers</title>
<script type='text/javascript' language='Javascript'>
<!--
var greatcomposersON = new Image;
var bachON = new Image;
var mozartON = new Image;
var beethovenON = new Image;

var greatcomposersOFF = new Image;
var bachOFF = new Image;
var mozartOFF = new Image;
var beethovenOFF = new Image;

greatcomposersON.src = "images/greatcomposerson.jpg";
bachON.src = "images/bachon.jpg";
mozartON.src = "images/mozarton.jpg";
beethovenON.src = "images/beethovenon.jpg";

greatcomposersOFF.src = "images/greatcomposersoff.jpg";
bachOFF.src = "images/bachoff.jpg";
mozartOFF.src = "images/mozartoff.jpg";
beethovenOFF.src = "images/beethovenoff.jpg";

function swapImage(version, imagename){
   if (document.images){
     document[imagename].src = ¬
eval(imagename + version + ".src");
   }
}

function rollOffAll(){
   swapImage('OFF','greatcomposers');
   swapImage('OFF','bach');
   swapImage('OFF','mozart');
   swapImage('OFF','beethoven');
}
//-->
```

> This function takes two parameters, the version name (ON or OFF) and the image name. This makes it possible to handle all image swapping with only this one function.

> This function turns all images back to their 'off' versions.

```
</script>
</head>
<body bgcolor="white">
<div align="center">
<a href="greatcomposers.html" onmouseover=
"swapImage('ON','greatcomposers');" onmouseout=
"rollOffAll();"
onclick="rollOffAll();return true;">
<img src="images/greatcomposersoff.jpg" width="250"
height="40" name="greatcomposers" border="0"
alt="Great Composers"></a>

<hr>
<br>
<a href="bach.html" onmouseover="swapImage('ON','bach');"
onmouseout="rollOffAll();"
onclick="rollOffAll();return true;"><img
src="images/bachoff.jpg" width="250" height="70"
name="bach" border="0" alt="Bach"></a><br>
<a href="mozart.html"
onmouseover="swapImage ('ON','mozart');"
onmouseout="rollOffAll();" onclick="rollOffAll();return
true;">
<img src="images/mozartoff.jpg" width="250" height="70"
name="mozart" border="0" alt="Mozart"></a><br>
<a href="beethoven.html"
onmouseover="swapImage('ON','beethoven');"
onmouseout="rollOffAll();" onclick="rollOffAll();return
true;">
<img src="images/beethovenoff.jpg" width="250"
height="70" name="beethoven" border="0" alt="Beethoven">
</a><br>
</div>
</body>
</html>
```

Listing 4.4 Multiple Rollover Images

Figure 4.2 shows the screen.

Figure 4.2 Output of Listing 4.4

How Does It Work?

Listing 4.4 produces the following sequence of events. Take your time and examine each step as it relates to the code.

1. The browser loads the HEAD portion of the HTML document into its memory.

2. The browser creates eight blank image objects with names corresponding to the on and off states of the four images on the page.

3. The browser fills the SRC properties of the new images by retrieving graphics files found in the images folder located in the same folder as the current document. The image files are now located in the browser's cache folder on the visitor's hard drive.

4. The browser loads the swapImage() and rollOffAll() functions into memory, but these functions do nothing until they are called.

5. The browser loads the BODY section of the document, including four named image objects created with the IMG tag.

6. The visitor moves the mouse on top of the image called beethoven. A mouseover event is generated in the browser's memory.

7. The anchor tag handles the mouseover event by calling the functionswapImage() and passing the desired version, ON, and the name of the image, beethoven, to the function.

8. The `swapImage()` function takes the name of the image `beethoven` and puts it into a variable called `imagename`. It then uses the `eval()` function to combine `imagename` with version (ON) and `.src` to produce `beethovenON.src`. The `eval()` function takes the contents of `beethovenON.src` (an image file) and assigns it to replace the SRC property of the `beethoven` image object. The image swap on rollover is accomplished.

9. The visitor moves the mouse outside the image, and the `onmouseout` event handler calls the `rollOffAll()` function. The `rollOffAll()` function calls the `swapImage()` function four times to change each image back to its off version.

10. The visitor rolls the mouse over any image. The `mouseover` and `mouseout` events are handled as described earlier. Glowing versions of each image appear on rollover.

11. The visitor clicks the `bach` image with the intention of viewing a related page about J.S. Bach.

12. The browser handles the click event by calling the `rollOffAll()` function. All the images revert to their `off` versions.

13. The `onclick` event handler returns a value of `true`, and that allows the browser to continue its normal link behavior and load the new Web page indicated in the HREF property of the `<a>` tag.

> ☆**TIP** `rollOffAll()` is particularly useful when you're using this page in a frameset.

◉◎ Creating a Double Rollover

The classic rollover technique is a nice interface enhancement. It provides feedback to visitors as they move the mouse. An even more useful enhancement gives visitors additional information about each link each time the mouse is rolled on top of the linked image. This technique can be called a **double rollover** because rolling the mouse over a linked image results in two image swaps rather than one.

Listing 4.5 creates the same rollover effects as Listing 4.4 but also displays image files of the birth and death dates of each composer.

```
<html><head><title>Rollover Composers</title>
<script type='text/javascript' language='Javascript'>
<!--
var greatcomposersON = new Image;
var bachON = new Image;
var mozartON = new Image;
var beethovenON = new Image;

var greatcomposersOFF = new Image;
var bachOFF = new Image;
```

```
var mozartOFF = new Image;
var beethovenOFF = new Image;

var greatcomposersINFO = new Image;
var bachINFO = new Image;
var mozartINFO = new Image;
var beethovenINFO = new Image;

greatcomposersON.src = "images/greatcomposerson.jpg";
bachON.src = "images/bachon.jpg";
mozartON.src = "images/mozarton.jpg";
beethovenON.src = "images/beethovenon.jpg";

greatcomposersOFF.src = "images/greatcomposersoff.jpg";
bachOFF.src = "images/bachoff.jpg";
mozartOFF.src = "images/mozartoff.jpg";
beethovenOFF.src = "images/beethovenoff.jpg";

greatcomposersINFO.src = "images/info.jpg";
bachINFO.src = "images/bachinfo.jpg";
mozartINFO.src = "images/mozartinfo.jpg";
beethovenINFO.src = "images/beethoveninfo.jpg";

function swapImage(version, imagename){
   if (document.images){
      document[imagename].src = eval(imagename + ¬
version + ".src");
      document['info'].src = eval(imagename + "INFO.src");
   }
}
```

This statement makes the info version of each image appear at the bottom of the page.

```
function rollOffAll(){
   swapImage('OFF','bach');
   swapImage('OFF','mozart');
   swapImage('OFF','beethoven');
   swapImage('OFF','greatcomposers');
}
//-->
</script>
</head>
<body bgcolor="white">
<div align="center">
```

Turns all images back to their 'off' versions. The greatcomposers image is turned off last because its associated INFO image is blank.

```
<a href="greatcomposers.html"
onmouseover="swapImage('ON','greatcomposers');" ¬
onmouseout="rollOffAll();" onclick="rollOffAll();return
true;">
<img src="images/greatcomposersoff.jpg" width="250"
height="40" name="greatcomposers" border="0" alt="Great
Composers"></a>
<hr>
<br>
<a href="bach.html" onmouseover="swapImage('ON','bach');"
onmouseout="rollOffAll();" onclick="rollOffAll();return ¬
true;">
<img src="images/bachoff.jpg" width="250" height="70"
name="bach" border="0" alt="Bach"></a><br>
<a href="mozart.html"
onmouseover="swapImage('ON','mozart');"
onmouseout="rollOffAll();" onclick="rollOffAll();return ¬
true;">
<img src="images/mozartoff.jpg" width="250" height="70"
name="mozart"border="0" alt="Mozart"></a><br>
<a href="beethoven.html"
onmouseover="swapImage('ON','beethoven');"
onmouseout="rollOffAll();" onclick="rollOffAll();return ¬
true;">
<img src="images/beethovenoff.jpg" width="250"
height="70" name="beethoven" border="0"
alt="Beethoven"></a><br>
<hr>
<a href="#" onmouseover="rollOffAll();"
onmouseout="rollOffAll();"
onclick="rollOffAll();return false;">
<img src="images/info.jpg" width="250" height="40"
name="info" border="0" alt="Dates"></a>
</div>
</body>
</html>
```

Listing 4.5 A Double Rollover

Figure 4.3 shows the screen.

Figure 4.3 Output of Listing 4.5

Here are the most significant differences between Listings 4.5 and 4.4:

☆ A fifth image has been added to the bottom of the page after the final `<hr>` tag. The image file `images/info.jpg` is a blank white rectangle 250 pixels wide by 40 pixels high. The name property of the `IMG` tag designates this image as `info`.

☆ Each `onmouseover` event handler calls the `swapImage()` function in Listing 4.5. The call sends the value `ON` as the version and the composer name as the image name. The `swapImage()` function changes the image file of the image with the corresponding composer name to show the glowing `ON` version. The `swapImage()` function changes the image file associated with the image called `info` to display the appropriate image file containing the birth and death dates of the composer.

☆ Each `onmouseout` event handler calls the `rollOffAll()` function to restore the `SRC` property of all the image objects, including the `info` image object, to the `off` versions.

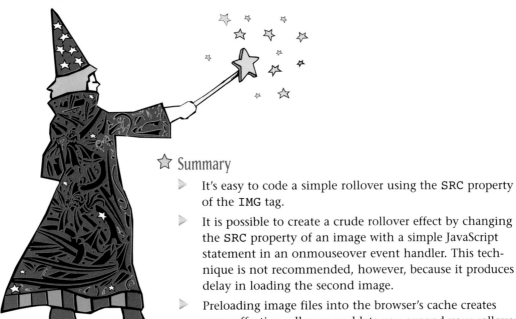

☆ Summary

▷ It's easy to code a simple rollover using the SRC property of the IMG tag.

▷ It is possible to create a crude rollover effect by changing the SRC property of an image with a simple JavaScript statement in an onmouseover event handler. This technique is not recommended, however, because it produces a delay in loading the second image.

▷ Preloading image files into the browser's cache creates more effective rollovers and lets you expand your rollover code to accommodate multiple rollover images or even double rollovers. Testing for the presence of the document.images array is an easy way to ensure that only those browsers that support the Image object will attempt to run your image swapping code.

▷ By passing parameter values, you can effect many types of rollover image swaps using a single function.

▷ A double rollover changes two image files when the mouse is rolled on top of each image. This interface enhancement gives the visitor additional information about each link when the mouse rolls over the linked image.

☆ Online References

W3Schools.com has an interesting example of image swapping that uses a button to change the image.
http://www.w3schools.com/dhtml/tryit.asp?filename=try_dom_image_src

Dr. Estrella's Interactive Web Programming. This site contains examples of image swapping and tutorials on understanding graphic manipulation for the Web. Look in the "Scripts to Study" and "Review" sections for examples.
http://www.stevenestrella.com/IWP

☆ Review Questions

1. An image object named beethoven can be referred to in JavaScript as document.beethoven or document['beethoven']. Why is the second form preferable?

2. Why are mouse event handlers placed in the <a> tag instead of the <img> tag?

3. When you add mouseover and mouseout event handlers to your HTML, what is the proper capitalization?

4. At what point in the loading of a Web page do the image files for rollover graphics actually get downloaded into the cache folder of the visitor's hard drive?

5. How can you ensure compatibility with very old browsers that do not support the Image object?

6. What property of the array object contains the number of elements in the array?

7. Why might you wish to create a page with a double rollover?

☆ Hands-On Exercises

1. Create a set of four pages using the HTML Builder from Chapter 2.

2. Set up the first page as the Great Composers home page with any text you like. Create three additional pages with text relating to Bach, Mozart, and Beethoven.

3. Create a frameset with a left frame called "navigation" 300 pixels wide and a right frame called "content" 500 pixels wide.

4. Load the double rollover page from Listing 4.5 into the navigation frame. Load your new Great Composers page into the content frame.

5. Change the links in the navigation frame to target the content frame (target = "content"), and test your new Web site.

CHAPTER FIVE

MORE IMAGE SWAPPING

In Chapter Four you learned basic image swapping techniques and applied them to create rollover images. Now you'll combine those techniques with others to create slide shows and animated banner advertisements.

Chapter Objectives

☆ To understand how to create captioned slide shows controlled by navigation buttons

☆ To learn how to create animated banner advertisements and link the banner images to various Web addresses

◎◎ Creating a Slide Show

To create slide shows on the Web, you preload a set of images, which are then displayed on demand as the visitor clicks forward and back buttons. Then, using techniques you learned in Chapter Three, you can add captions to your slide show. You can use the slide show technique whenever you need to present a sequence of images with accompanying text. For example, you could use a series of slides to demonstrate the steps involved in preparing a recipe, assembling a bicycle, or learning a dance routine.

Listing 5.1 creates a slide show of my trip to India. Captions appear in a text field below each image.

```
<html><head><title>Sample Slide Show</title>
<script language="JAVASCRIPT" type="text/javascript">
<!--
var mySlides = new Array();       Here the image objects
mySlides[1] = new Image();        are stored in an array.
mySlides[2] = new Image();
mySlides[3] = new Image();
mySlides[4] = new Image();
mySlides[5] = new Image();
mySlides[6] = new Image();

mySlides[1].src = "images/indiaflag.jpg";
mySlides[2].src = "images/snakecharmer.jpg";
mySlides[3].src = "images/tajmahal.jpg";
mySlides[4].src = "images/jaipurrugs.jpg";
mySlides[5].src = "images/jagmandir.jpg";
mySlides[6].src = "images/jaintemple.jpg";

var myCaptions = new Array();      The text captions are stored in another array.
myCaptions[1] = "The flag of India is saffron, white, ¬
and green. ";
myCaptions[1] += "Each color has philosophical ¬
significance.";
myCaptions[2] = "We arrived in Delhi and actually saw ¬
a snake charmer.";
myCaptions[3] = "The Taj Mahal in Agra is ¬
overwhelming.";
myCaptions[4] = "Rugs made in India are quite complex ¬
and beautiful.";
myCaptions[5] = "Jag Mandir in Udaipur was in a James ¬
Bond movie.";
myCaptions[6] = "The inside of a Jain Temple.";

var slidenumber = 1;
var totalslides = mySlides.length - 1;
```

```
function showSlide(direction){
  if (direction == "next"){
    (slidenumber == totalslides) ? slidenumber = 1 : ¬
slidenumber++;
  }else{
    (slidenumber == 1) ? slidenumber = totalslides : ¬
slidenumber--;
  }
  if (document.images){
    document.slideframe.src = mySlides[slidenumber].src;
    document.slidecontrols.caption.value = ¬
myCaptions[slidenumber];
    document.slidecontrols.currentslide.value = ¬
slidenumber;
  }
}
//-->
</script>
</head>
<body bgcolor="white">
<div align="CENTER">
<h2>Photos from our trip to India</h2>

<img src="images/indiaflag.jpg" name="slideframe"
width="320"
height="240" alt="Slide show images appear here.">

<form name="slidecontrols">
<p><textarea name="caption" rows="2" cols="50">Our slide
show begins with the flag of India.</textarea><br>
<br>
<input type="button" value="Previous Slide"
onclick="showSlide('previous');">
<input type="button" value="Next Slide"
onclick="showSlide('next');"><br>
<br>
Slide Number:
<input type="TEXT" value="1" name="currentslide"
size="5"></p>
</form>
</div>
</body>
</html>
```

Listing 5.1 A Slide Show

> ☆**SHORTCUT**   **If-Else Made Easier**
>
> The `showSlide()` function introduces a shortcut form of the if-else structure that uses the conditional operator (the question mark).
>
> `(slidenumber == totalslides) ? slidenumber = 1 : slidenumber++;`
>
> Everything before the question mark is the **condition**. If the condition is true, the statement before the colon (`:`) is executed. Otherwise, the statement after the colon is executed.

Figure 5.1 shows the output of Listing 5.1.

Figure 5.1 Output of Listing 5.1

How Does It Work?

1. The browser loads the HEAD and stores six new image objects in an array called `mySlides` beginning at array element 1. The SRC property of each image is filled with a `.jpg` file located in the images folder. This step effectively preloads all the images.

☆**TIP**   Note that each image in the series must be exactly the same width and height.

2. The browser stores all the captions in an array called `myCaptions` beginning with array element 1. Each caption is a simple text string. Notice the use of the add-by-value operator (`+=`) to store the long caption for the first image in `myCaptions[1]`.

3. A global variable, `slidenumber`, is created to hold the number of the current slide. A second global variable, `totalslides`, is created to hold the number of slides in the presentation. Because element 0 of the `mySlides` array is not used, we must subtract 1 from the length of the array to determine the number of slides.

4. The function `showSlide(direction)` is stored in memory and will perform its tasks when called upon later.

5. The `BODY` of the document includes an image called `slideframe` and a `FORM` called `slidecontrols`. Within the `FORM` is a `TEXTAREA` called `caption` set to display 2 rows and 50 columns of text. An initial text string informs the visitor that the slide show begins with the flag of India. The `FORM` also includes two buttons. The first button calls the `showSlide()` function and sends it the value `previous`. The second button calls the `showSlide()` function and sends it the value `next`.

6. The `showSlide()` function in the `HEAD` takes the value of the parameter it receives (`previous` or `next`) and places it in a temporary variable called `direction`. If `direction` is `next`, the function looks to see whether the current slide number (stored in the global variable `slidenumber`) is the last slide in the series. If it is, `slidenumber` is reset to 1. Otherwise, `slidenumber` is incremented by 1. If `direction` is `previous`, the function looks to see whether the current slide number (stored in the global variable `slidenumber`) is the first slide in the series. If it is, `slidenumber` is set to the total number of slides. Otherwise, `slidenumber` is decremented by 1. With this technique, the slide show wraps around from the last image to the first.

7. The `showSlide()` function checks to make sure that the browser supports the `images` array. It then uses the current value of `slidenumber` to determine which element of the `mySlides` array and which element of the `myCaptions` array to display. Finally, `slidenumber` is also displayed in the text field called `currentslide` so that the visitor will see the number of the current slide.

This slide show technique is useful for building pages where you want the visitor to proceed through a series of images by clicking buttons. Corporate presentations, travel logs, and instructional demonstrations are some of the possible applications. Sometimes, however, it's desirable for the images to change at predetermined intervals to produce an animation. We take a look at that next.

Creating Animated Advertising Banners

During the dot-com mania of the late 1990s, a new form of advertising was born. Animated **banner advertising** images were created to encourage Web page visitors to link to sites displaying related information or products. For example, let's look at a page about music history that has an ad banner to encourage the visitor to use an online dictionary of composers. The banner consists of the dictionary's logo followed by a series of three composer names. If the visitor clicks on the dictionary logo, the dictionary home page loads. If the visitor clicks on a composer name, the appropriate biography page loads. Listing 5.2 demonstrates this ad banner using some familiar image files from Chapter Four.

```
<html><head><title>Rotating Ad Banner</title>
<script language="JAVASCRIPT" type="text/javascript">
<!--
var myAds = new Array();
myAds[1] = new Image();
myAds[2] = new Image();
myAds[3] = new Image();
myAds[4] = new Image();

myAds[1].src = "images/composerdictionary.jpg";
myAds[2].src = "images/bachoff.jpg";
myAds[3].src = "images/mozartoff.jpg";
myAds[4].src = "images/beethovenoff.jpg";

var myTimings = new Array();
myTimings[1] = 3000;
myTimings[2] = 1500;
myTimings[3] = 1500;
myTimings[4] = 1500;

var mySites = new Array();
mySites[1] = "http://www.stevenestrella.com/composers";
mySites[2] = "http://www.stevenestrella.com/composers/¬
bach.html";
mySites[3] = "http://www.stevenestrella.com/composers/¬
mozart.html";
mySites[4] = "http://www.stevenestrella.com/composers/¬
beethoven.html";
```

The timings represent the number of milliseconds delay between the images.

```
var adnumber = 0;
var totalads = myAds.length - 1;
var timerID = "";

function startBanner(){
  adnumber = 0;
  showAd();
}
function showAd(){
  if (document.images){
    if (document.myBanner.complete){
      adnumber++;
      (adnumber > totalads) ? adnumber=1 : ¬
adnumber=adnumber;
      document.myBanner.src = myAds[adnumber].src;
    }
    timerID = setTimeout("showAd()", ¬
myTimings[adnumber]);
  }
}
function goSite(){
  clearTimeout(timerID);
  window.location.href = mySites[adnumber];
}
//-->
</script>
</head>
<body bgcolor="#FFFFFF" onload="startBanner();">
<div align="CENTER">
<a href="http://www.stevenestrella.com/composers"
onclick="goSite();return false;">
<img src="images/composerdictionary.jpg"
name="myBanner" width="250" height="70" border="0"
alt="composer dictionary"></a></div>
</body>
</html>
```

> This condition ensures that each image loads completely before the next image appears in the sequence.

> Older browsers ignore the onclick handler and load the URL from the HREF attribute. Newer browsers support the onclick handler and call the goSite() function to load the appropriate URL. The statement return false; ensures that the URL from the HREF attribute will NOT be loaded on new browsers.

Listing 5.2 An Animated Banner Advertisement

Figure 5.2 shows the output of Listing 5.2.

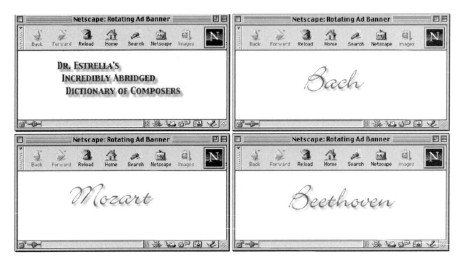

Figure 5.2 Output of Listing 5.2 with All Four Images

☆ **TIP**   Using the `setTimeout()` method

The window object created by most browsers can perform actions known as methods. One method you've encountered in earlier examples is the alert method. The formal statement of this method, `window.alert()`, would include the object name, but in practice the name of the window object is assumed.

```
alert('Some message here.')
```

The `setTimeout()` method of the window object lets you execute a JavaScript function after a delay (in milliseconds) of your choosing. You can think of the `setTimeout()` method as a way to schedule a task for the browser to perform. The `setTimeout()` method generates an ID number to identify the task. It's best to store this ID in a variable so that you can later cancel the scheduled task with a call to the `clearTimeout()` method.

```
var timerID = setTimeout('somefunction()',delayvariable);
```

In this case, if `delayvariable` is set to 1000, `somefunction()` will execute after a one-second delay. The task is assigned a number and stored in `timerID`. To cancel this task, use the `clearTimeout` method and the `timerID`.

```
clearTimeout(timerID);
```

How Does It Work?

1. The browser loads the HEAD and creates four new image objects in an array called `myAds`. The SRC property of each image is preloaded with a `.jpg` file located in the `images` folder. Each image is the same width and height.

2. The browser stores timings for the slide show in an array called `myTimings`. The values are in milliseconds. For example, the value 3000 in `myTimings[1]` indicates a delay of 3 seconds between the appearance of image 1 and the appearance of image 2.

3. The `mySites` array stores Web addresses that will be linked to the images.

4. A global variable, `adnumber`, is created to hold the number of the current image. A second global variable, `totalads`, is created to hold the number of images in the animation. Because element 0 of the myAds array is not used, we must subtract 1 from the length of the array to determine the number of images. A third global variable, `timerID`, is initialized here for later use.

5. The functions `showAd()` and `goSite()` are stored in memory and will perform their tasks when called upon later.

6. The BODY of the document includes an image called `myBanner` surrounded by an anchor tag (`<a></a>`). Version 4.0 and later Web browsers recognize the `onclick` handler in the anchor tag. Earlier browsers ignore it but recognize the HREF property.

7. When the page finishes loading, the LOAD event occurs. The window object will react to the LOAD event if an `onload` event handler is present in the BODY tag. In this example, the `onload` handler calls the `startBanner()` function, which sets the `adnumber` variable to 0 and calls the `showAd()` function to start the banner animation.

8. The `showAd()` function in the HEAD checks first to make sure that the images array is supported by the browser. It then checks to make sure that the current image is complete; it makes little sense to begin loading image 2 if image 1 has not been displayed. The global variable `adnumber` is incremented by 1. Then `adnumber` is tested to see whether it is larger than totalads. If it is, `adnumber` is reset to 1 and the animation begins again at the first image. The value in `adnumber` determines which image file gets loaded into the SRC property of `myBanner`.

9. The `setTimeout()` method calls the `showAd()` function repeatedly. The delay between calls is determined by the value of element `adnumber` of the `myTimings` array. In this way, the timing between images can vary according to the image content. For example, you can set images having more text to a longer delay, thereby allowing time for the visitor to read the text. A unique ID number is stored in the global variable `timerID` for each task scheduled by the `setTimeout()` method.

10. The visitor clicks on the Bach image, the second image in the series. At that moment the value of `adnumber` is 2. A click event is generated. The `onclick` event handler in the anchor tag surrounding the image responds to the click event by calling the `goSite()` function.

11. The goSite() function stops the banner animation using the clearTimeout() method. The goSite() function passes the timerID variable, which tells the clearTimeout() method which task to cancel.

12. The goSite() function changes the href property of the location object of the current window to the Web address stored in element adnumber of the mySites array. Because adnumber is currently 2, the Bach page loads in the current window. This works because the location object represents the URL currently loaded in the window. If the href property of the location object is changed to a different URL, the new URL is automatically loaded.

☆ Summary

▷ The technique of preloading multiple images can be applied to creating slide shows. Image swapping may be triggered by a variety of events. Mouseover events are common triggers but CLICK events work just as well. Buttons or links with onclick handlers may then be used to trigger image swaps. If a function accepts parameters, its behavior will vary depending on the value of the parameter. A function to change images in a slide show may do one thing if the parameter next is received and another if the parameter previous is received.

▷ An advertising banner with images that change according to a schedule is one use of the setTimeout() method. This method of the window object allows you to schedule tasks for the Web browser to perform after a given delay. A unique number for each requested task may be stored in a variable so that the task may be cancelled using the clearTimeout() method.

☆ Online References

Raymond Camden has published a slide show template that is free for nonprofit and education use.
http://www.camdenfamily.com/morpheus/slide/

The Maricopa Center for Learning and Instruction has published a useful slide show template consisting of several HTML files and some JavaScript.
http://www.mcli.dist.maricopa.edu/proj/jclicker/

Webreference.com has a helpful tutorial on creating rotating text banners.
http://www.webreference.com/js/column3/

ZDNet developer's site presents a slight variant of the rotating image banner technique explained in this chapter.
http://www.zdnet.com/devhead/stories/articles/ ¬
0,4413,2422293,00.html

CNET's builder site has helpful articles on creating graphics for use on the Web.
http://builder.cnet.com/

☆ Review Questions

1. What code must you add to a button on a form so that it will perform a function when clicked?

2. What is the conditional operator? Give an example.

3. What is a parameter, and how do you pass one?

4. What object uses the `setTimeout()` method?

5. What does the `clearTimeout()` method do?

6. How do you start a banner animation as soon as the page loads?

7. How do you change the page currently displayed?

☆ Hands-On Exercises

1. Create a slide show with navigation buttons and text fields.

2. Create an animated banner and link the images to your favorite Web sites.

3. Combine elements of Exercises 1 and 2 to create a variant of the slide show that allows the visitor to choose the image to be displayed. Use a table of links on the bottom of the screen and a single large image on the top. When the visitor clicks each link, a different image replaces the one already displayed. Each link should contain an onclick handler to call the image swapping function.

CHAPTER SIX

WORKING WITH DATES AND TIMES

One easy way to add dynamic content to your Web pages is to base the content on the current date or time. Your Web page might display a clock that updates each second, or it might greet visitors with a different message depending on the time of day. You can also produce interesting pages by allowing visitors to make simple date and time calculations. Perhaps your visitor would be interested to know that a famous person was born on the visitor's birthday or that the current time in New Zealand is 2 AM.

Chapter Objectives

☆ To understand JavaScript's Date object

☆ To learn how to add a clock to a Web page

☆ To find out how to display the time and date in any format you like

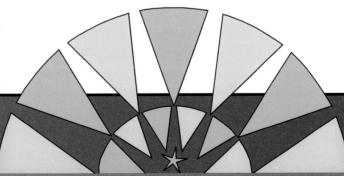

☆ To see how to add a greeting to a Web page that changes with the time of day

☆ To learn how to add a time-sensitive greeting to your Web page clock

☆ To discover how to perform calculations based on dates

◎◎ The Date Object

JavaScript works with objects in a host environment, typically a Web browser. By now you're familiar with the window, document, form, and image objects. The browser creates these objects. The Date object, however, is one of a handful of core objects that exists in the JavaScript language independently of the host environment. If all you ever do with JavaScript is to create Web pages, this distinction isn't terribly important. JavaScript is increasing in popularity, however, and this means your new skills in JavaScript programming will be valuable in scripting the objects of other host environments you'll encounter.

To use the Date object you must first create an instance of it in memory.

```
var currentDate = new Date();
```

The variable `currentDate` now contains a number equal to the number of milliseconds that have elapsed since midnight of January 1, 1970. Dates before 1970 are represented as negative milliseconds.

After you create an instance of the `Date()` object, you can apply a variety of methods to determine the current minute, hour, second, month, and so on. Following are some common Date methods:

☆ `currentDate.getDate()` returns the date (1–31) of the month.

☆ `currentDate.getDay()` returns the day of the week (0–6 for Sunday through Saturday).

☆ `currentDate.getFullYear()` returns the four-digit year (for example, 2001).

☆ `currentDate.getHours()` returns the hour (0–23).

☆ `currentDate.getMilliseconds()` returns the milliseconds elapsed since the last second (0–999).

☆ `currentDate.getMinutes()` returns the minutes elapsed since the last hour (0–59).

☆ `currentDate.getMonth()` returns the month (0–11 for January through December).

☆ `currentDate.getSeconds()` returns the seconds elapsed since the last minute (0–59).

☆ `currentDate.getTime()` returns the milliseconds elapsed since January 1, 1970.

☆ currentDate.getYear() returns the two-digit year (for example, 01). This method was common before 2000 but has since been replaced with the getFullYear() method.

☆ currentDate.toLocaleString() expresses the date and time as text formatted to local standards (for example, "Tuesday, 31 July, 2001 11:03:19 AM").

Notice that the getDate() method returns the date in a range of 1 to 31. Most of the other methods return zero-based information. For example, zero represents January in the getMonth() method. Note that the values returned by the Date() object are only as accurate as the clock on the visitor's computer.

◉◉ Creating a Simple Clock

Listing 6.1 demonstrates how easy it is to add a simple clock to a Web page.

```
<html><head><title>Basic Clock</title>
<script type="text/javascript" language="JavaScript">
<!--
function showTime(){
    var now = new Date();
    document.clock.face.value = now.toLocaleString();
}
//-->
</script>
</head>
<body bgcolor="white"
onload="setInterval('showTime()',1000);">
<div align="CENTER">
<h1>A Very Basic JavaScript Clock</h1>

<form name="clock"><input name="face" size="50"></form>
</div>
</body>
</html>
```

A new Date() object is created and stored in a variable.

The toLocaleString() method of the Date object converts the date to a text format used in the visitor's location.

The setInterval() method causes the clock to be updated every second.

Listing 6.1 A Simple Clock

☆**TIP**   Using the setInterval() Method

The setInterval() method of the window object is very similar to the setTimeout() method. The setTimeout() method schedules a task to be executed *once* after a given delay. The setInterval() method schedules a task to be executed *repeatedly* with a given delay between repetitions. The setInterval() method is ideal for generating a clock that updates every second (1000 milliseconds) and is supported by browsers with version numbers 4 and higher.

Figure 6.1 shows the output of Listing 6.1.

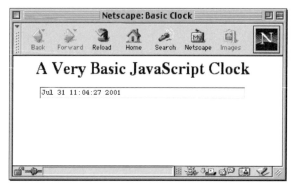

Figure 6.1 Output of Listing 6.1 in Internet Explorer (top) and Netscape

How Does It Work?

1. The page loads, and the `setInterval()` method begins to call the `showTime()` function repeatedly every 1000 milliseconds.

2. Each time the `showTime()` function is called, the variable `now` is created as an instance of the `Date` object.

3. The `toLocaleString()` method is applied to the `now` date object.

4. The result is displayed in a field called `face` on a form called `clock`. The exact form of the date and time will vary depending on location, browser, and operating system. Figure 6.1 shows the output in Internet Explorer 5 (top) and Netscape Communicator 4.7 on a Macintosh.

It's easy to implement Listing 6.1 on a Web page, but it gives you little control over the format of the date and time. For example, the `toLocaleString()` method shows both the date and the time, but you may wish to display only the time. Some browsers and operating systems will display military time, and others will display U.S. time (AM and PM). Fortunately, you can exercise more control over dates and times, as discussed next.

◎◎ Creating a Better Clock

Listing 6.2 demonstrates one way to add a customized clock to your Web page.

```
<html><head><title>A Better Clock</title>
<script type="text/javascript" language="JavaScript">
<!--
var timerID = "";
function startClock(){
    timerID = setInterval('showTime()',1000);
}
function stopClock(){
    clearInterval(timerID);
}
function showTime(){
    var now = new Date();
    var hours = now.getHours();
    var minutes = now.getMinutes();
    var seconds = now.getSeconds();
```

> `getHours()`, `getMinutes()`, and `getSeconds()` are built-in methods of the Date object.

```
    /* This routine adds leading zeroes when needed. */
    var timeValue = hours > 12 ? hours - 12 : hours;
    timeValue == 0 ? timeValue = 12 : timeValue;
    timeValue  += minutes < 10 ? ":0" : ":";
    timeValue  += minutes;
    timeValue  += seconds < 10 ? ":0" : ":";
    timeValue  += seconds;
    timeValue  += hours >= 12 ? " PM" : " AM";
    document.clock.face.value = timeValue;
}
//-->
</script>
</head>
```

> The `startClock()` function is called when the document is completely loaded in the browser window.

```
<body bgcolor="white" onload="startClock();">
<div align="CENTER">
<h1>A Better Clock</h1>

<form name="clock"><input name="face" size="15"><br>
<br>
<input type="button" name="startclock"
value="Start Clock" onclick="startClock();">
<input type="button" name="stopclock" value="Stop Clock"
onclick="stopClock();"></form>
</div>
</body>
</html>
```

Listing 6.2 A Customized Clock

Figure 6.2 shows the output of Listing 6.2.

Figure 6.2 Output of Listing 6.2

How Does It Work?

1. The page loads, a global variable for `timerID` is created, a few functions load into memory, and the onload handler in the `BODY` tag calls the `startClock()` function.

2. The `startClock()` function begins. The `setInterval()` method calls the `showTime()` function repeatedly every 1000 milliseconds. Each time the `setInterval()` method is called, it generates an ID number that is stored in `timerID`.

3. The `showTime()` function creates the variable `now` as an instance of the `Date` object. New variables to hold the current hour, minutes, and seconds are also created and filled using the appropriate `Date` methods.

4. A variable called `timeValue` is created to hold the current time formatted as hours, minutes, and seconds with AM or PM as needed. The conditional operator (`?`) is used to determine whether the minutes and seconds need leading zeroes and whether the hour is in the AM or PM.

5. The result is displayed in a field called `face` on a `form` called `clock`. The form of this clock will be consistent across browsers and platforms.

6. Two buttons at the bottom of the page call the `startClock()` and `stopClock()` functions to allow the visitor to control the clock display. The `stopClock()` function uses the `clearInterval()` method of the `window` object to prevent any further calls to the `showTime()` function.

Listing 6.2 takes more time to implement than Listing 6.1 but gives you much more control.

Creating Dynamic Greetings

Now that you know how to determine the time, it might be nice to greet your visitors appropriately. Listing 6.3 demonstrates one way to add a greeting that varies with the time of day.

```html
<html><head><title>Dynamic Greeting</title>
<script type="text/javascript" language="JavaScript">
<!--
var now = new Date();
var hours = now.getHours();
var greeting = "";
if (hours <= 24) { greeting = "Good evening"; }
if (hours <= 17) { greeting = "Good afternoon"; }
if (hours <= 11) { greeting = "Good morning"; }
if (hours <= 4) { greeting = "Isn't it past your ¬
bedtime?"; }
//-->
</script>
</head>
<body bgcolor="white">
<div align="CENTER">
<h1>Dynamic Greetings</h1>

<h2>
<script type="text/javascript" language="JAVASCRIPT">
<!--
document.write(greeting);
//-->
</script>
</h2>

<p>The greeting above was generated with JavaScript
based on the time of day.</p>
</div>
</body>
</html>
```

The greeting is chosen based on the value of hours.

A script in the body writes the greeting as the document loads.

Listing 6.3 A Dynamic Greeting

Figure 6.3 shows the output of Listing 6.3.

Figure 6.3 Output of Listing 6.3

How Does It Work?

1. The HEAD portion of the page loads. Because there are no functions in the HEAD, all the JavaScript statements execute as soon as the page loads. First, a new Date object is created named now.

2. Global variables are created to hold the current hour and the greeting.

3. A series of conditional structures tests the hour to select the appropriate greeting.

4. The BODY begins to load. A level 1 heading appears.

5. A level 2 heading follows. The text of the level 2 heading is created with a script.

6. The script uses the write() method of the document object to add the greeting that was selected in the HEAD.

7. The rest of the document loads normally.

> ☆ **TIP**   Scripts in the BODY?
>
> You can include scripts in the BODY section of the document. Often, such scripts refer to variables and values already created in the HEAD. In Listing 6.3, the script works in the BODY because the global variable greeting was created in the HEAD.

Listing 6.3 has one disadvantage. After the page loads, the greeting is fixed. There is no setInterval() method to repeatedly update the time and greeting. If the visitor loads the page at 5:59 PM, the greeting will read "Good Afternoon." One minute later, when evening begins, the greeting will be outdated. It might also be nice to include the date in your greeting. Keep reading.

◎◎ Creating a Decision-Making Clock with Date

In Listing 6.4 the date and time are formatted in one long text string and displayed in a field. A second field displays a greeting that varies with the time of day and updates itself each second. When afternoon changes to evening, the greeting changes accordingly.

> ☆ **SHORTCUT**   The code in Listing 6.4 contains an array for the days of the week and a second array for the months of the year. To save time, you can copy these arrays into `mylibrary.js` for use in future pages.

```
<html><head><title>Decision Clock with Date</title>
<script type="text/javascript" language="JavaScript">
<!--
var theDays = new Array();      The array of days - store in mylibrary.js.
theDays[0]="Sunday";
theDays[1]="Monday";
theDays[2]="Tuesday";
theDays[3]="Wednesday";
theDays[4]="Thursday";
theDays[5]="Friday";
theDays[6]="Saturday";

var theMonths = new Array();     The array of months - store in mylibrary.js.
theMonths[0]="January";
theMonths[1]="February";
theMonths[2]="March";
theMonths[3]="April";
theMonths[4]="May";
theMonths[5]="June";
theMonths[6]="July";
theMonths[7]="August";
theMonths[8]="September";
theMonths[9]="October";
theMonths[10]="November";
theMonths[11]="December";

function showTime(){
    var now = new Date();
    var hours = now.getHours();
    var minutes = now.getMinutes();
    var seconds = now.getSeconds();

    var timeValue = "" + ((hours > 12) ? hours - 12 : ¬
hours);
```

```
        ((timeValue == 0) ? timeValue = 12 : timeValue);
        timeValue  += ((minutes < 10) ? ":0" : ":") + ¬
minutes;
        timeValue  += ((seconds < 10) ? ":0" : ":") + ¬
seconds;
        timeValue  += (hours >= 12) ? " PM" : " AM";

        var greeting = "";
        if (hours <= 24) { greeting = "Good evening."; }
        if (hours <= 17) { greeting = "Good afternoon."; }
        if (hours <= 11) { greeting = "Good morning."; }
        if (hours <= 4) { greeting = "Isn't it past your ¬
bedtime?"; }

        var theyear  = now.getFullYear();
        var themonth = now.getMonth();
        var thedate = now.getDate();
        var theday = now.getDay();

        var theLongDate = theDays[theday] + ", ";
        theLongDate += thedate + " " + theMonths[themonth];
        theLongDate += ", " + theyear;

        document.clock.calendarpage.value = theLongDate + ¬
" " + timeValue;
        document.clock.feedback.value = greeting;
}
//-->
</script>
</head>
<body bgcolor="white"
onload="setInterval('showTime()',1000);">
<div align="CENTER">
<h1>A Decision-Making Clock with Date</h1>

<form name="clock"><input name="calendarpage" size="45">
<br>
<input name="feedback" size="45"><br>
<br>
</form>
</div>
</body>
</html>
```

> Use getFullYear() to get the 4-digit year. The old getYear() method provided only a 2-digit year and caused problems when the century changed.

Listing 6.4 A Dynamic Greeting with Date

Figure 6.4 shows the output of Listing 6.4.

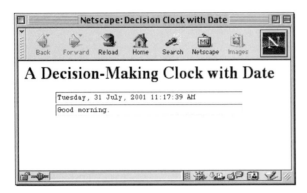

Figure 6.4 Output of Listing 6.4

How Does It Work?

1. The HEAD portion of the page loads. Two arrays are created to hold the names of the days of the week and the months. The numbering of these arrays begins at 0 to correspond to the number of the getDay() and getMonth() methods of the Date object. The showTime() function loads into memory.

☆SHORTCUT   The theDays and theMonths arrays will likely be used in many other pages, so it's a good idea to copy them into your external library, mylibrary.js.

2. The BODY loads a form having two fields called calendarpage and feedback to hold the date and the greeting. When the page has completely loaded, the onload handler in the BODY tag invokes the setInterval() method of the window object to repeatedly call the showTime() function once each second. Because this page includes no buttons to allow the user to stop the clock, it is not necessary to create a timerID variable.

3. The showTime() function creates the variable now as an instance of the Date object. New variables to hold the current hour, minutes, and seconds are also created and filled using the appropriate Date methods.

4. A variable called timeValue is created to hold the current time formatted as hours, minutes, and seconds with AM or PM as needed. A series of conditional structures tests the hour to select the appropriate greeting.

5. Four new variables are created to store the year, month, date, and day. These variables are filled using the date methods explained earlier. If the date is 31 July, 2001, then theyear would be 2001, themonth would be 6, thedate would be 31, and theday would be 2 (Tuesday).

6. A new variable called theLongDate is created to hold the text string expression of the date.

7. If the date is Tuesday, 31 July 2001 then `theday` would be 2 (Sunday = 0, Monday = 1, Tuesday = 2). Array element 2 of `theDays` is the text string `Tuesday`. A comma and space are added. On the next line we add the date (31 in our example), a space, and the current month name as found in the `theMonths` array. On the final line we add a comma, a space, and `theyear` (2001 in our example). The variable `theLongDate` now contains the text string `Tuesday, 31 July, 2001`.

8. The variable `theLongDate` is appended with the variable `timeValue` containing a formatted string of text such as `11:17:39 AM`. The result is displayed in a field called `calendarpage` on a form called `clock`. The greeting from step 4 appears in a field called `feedback` on the same form.

◎◎ Creating a Countdown Page

Now that you know some of the basics of working with dates and times, you can start to create interesting pages that provide useful information. Listing 6.9 uses basic math to create a page that calculates the number of seconds, minutes, hours, days, and years your visitor has left before retirement. The code in Listing 6.9 also uses the day and month arrays you created in Listing 6.7 and stored in your `mylibrary.js` file.

```
<html><head><title>Countdown to Retirement</title>
<script type="text/javascript" language="JAVASCRIPT" src=
"mylibrary.js">
</script>
```

> Be sure to properly reference your library.

```
<script type="text/javascript" language="JavaScript">
<!--
var birthyear = "";
var birthday = "";
var birthmonth = "";
var retirementyear = "";
var timerID = "";
var firstdate = new Date();
var lastdate = new Date();

function startClock(){
   var question1 = "Type the 4-digit year of your ¬
birth.";
   birthyear = window.prompt(question1,"1962");
   birthmonth = window.prompt("What month? (1-12) ¬
","9") - 1;
   birthday = window.prompt("What day? (1-31)","12");
   var question2 = "At what age do you plan to retire?";
   retirementage = window.prompt(question2,"65");
```

Create a Date object to hold the visitor's birthdate.

```
        firstdate = new Date(birthyear,birthmonth,birthday);
    retirementyear = parseInt(birthyear) + ¬
parseInt(retirementage);
    lastdate = new Date(retirementyear,birthmonth, ¬
birthday);
    timerID = setInterval('showTime()',1000);
}
function stopClock(){
    clearInterval(timerID);
}
function showTime(){
    var now = new Date();
    var seconds = (lastdate.getTime() - ¬
now.getTime())/1000;
    document.clock.secondsface.value = ¬
Math.round(seconds);
    document.clock.minutesface.value = ¬
Math.round(seconds/60);
    document.clock.hoursface.value = ¬
Math.round(seconds/60/60);
    document.clock.daysface.value = ¬
Math.round(seconds/60/60/24);
    document.clock.workdays.value = ¬
Math.round((seconds/60/60/24)*.65);
    document.clock.fundays.value = ¬
Math.round((seconds/60/60/24)*.35);
    document.clock.yearsface.value = ¬
Math.round(seconds/60/60/24/365.25);
    birthdatedisplay = theDays[firstdate.getDay()] + ",";
    birthdatedisplay += birthday + " ";
    birthdatedisplay += theMonths[birthmonth] + ", " + ¬
birthyear;

    retirementdisplay = theDays[lastdate.getDay()] + ",";
    retirementdisplay += birthday + " ";
    retirementdisplay += theMonths[birthmonth] + ", " + ¬
retirementyear;

    document.clock.birthdate.value = birthdatedisplay;
    document.clock.retirementdate.value = ¬
retirementdisplay;
}
//-->
</script>
</head>
<body bgcolor="white">
<h1>Retirement Countdown</h1>
```

Create a Date object to hold the visitor's retirement date.

The getDay() method determines the day of the week.

```
<form name="clock">
<p>Click the Start Clock button to begin. <input
type="button"
name="startclock" value="Start Clock"
onclick="startClock();">
<input type="button" name="stopclock" value="Stop Clock"
onclick="stopClock();"></p>

<p>Birth Date: <input name="birthdate" size="40"><br>
<br>
Retirement Date: <input name="retirementdate"
size="40"><br>
<br>
<b>Countdown to retirement:</b><br>
<br>
Seconds: <input name="secondsface" size="18"> Minutes:
<input name="minutesface" size="15"><br>
<br>
Hours: <input name="hoursface" size="13"> Days: <input
name="daysface" size="8"> Years: <input name="yearsface"
size="5"></p>

<p><b>Work Days versus Fun Days</b><br>
A typical full-time employee works 65 out of every 100
days.<br>
Work days left: <input name="workdays" size="10"> Fun
days before retirement: <input name="fundays"
size="10"></p>

<h2>Now that is something to think about!</h2>
</form>
</body>
</html>
```

Listing 6.5 A Countdown Page

☆ **TIP**   **Using the Math Object**

The Math object, like the Date object, is a core JavaScript object. The principal difference between the two is that the Math object is static, meaning that you never create instances of the Math object. Instead, think of it as JavaScript's built-in calculator. When you need to round a number use `Math.round(somenumber)`. Here are some of the other common methods of the Math object.

⋆ `Math.abs(x)` returns the absolute value of x.

⋆ `Math.floor(x)` returns the integer portion of x.

⋆ `Math.max(x,y)` returns the greater of x or y.

⋆ `Math.min(x,y)` returns the lesser of x or y.

⋆ `Math.random()` returns a random number between 0 and 1.

☆**WARNING** **Getting Numbers from Text Strings**

In Listing 6.9, the code

```
retirementyear = parseInt(birthyear) + parseInt(retirementage)
```

adds the visitor's age at retirement to the visitor's birth year. If the visitor was born in 1962 and intends to retire at age 65, the result should be 2027. The problem is that the values in birthyear and retirementage were obtained with window prompts and stored as text strings. Combining the text strings "1962" and "65" produces "196265", which would ensure our visitor great longevity but a long wait to retirement.

The `parseInt()` function is useful to convert text strings to integers when the first character is a numeric value. The expressions `parseInt("65a")` and `parseInt("65.75")` would both return the integer value of 65. The expression `parseInt("a65")` would return the value `NaN` to indicate that the value passed to the function was not a number. The `parseInt()` function **parses** (analyzes) the text string. Use the `parseInt()` function or the `parseFloat()` function (for values with numbers after the decimal point) whenever you have a text string that must be interpreted as a number. These are global functions built into JavaScript.

Using the `parseInt()` function in Listing 6.9, the numbers 1962 and 65 can be summed correctly and the visitor can retire in 2027.

Figure 6.5 shows the output of Listing 6.5.

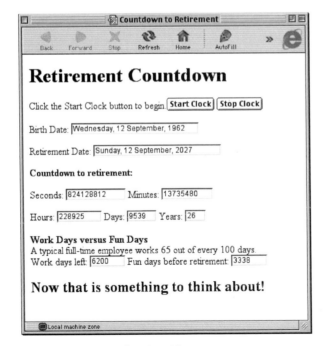

Figure 6.5 Output of Listing 6.5

How Does It Work?

1. The HEAD portion of the page loads. The external library, mylibrary.js, loads into memory. The arrays for the names of the days of the week and the months are stored there.

2. Global variables for the visitor's birth year, day, month, and retirement year are created. The familiar global variable timerID is also created to allow the visitor to control the countdown. Two new date objects are created. The one called firstdate will hold the visitor's birthdate. The one called lastdate will hold the visitor's date of retirement. The startClock(), stopClock(), and showTime() functions load into memory.

3. The BODY loads a form with several fields to hold the output of the showTime() function. The BODY also contains two buttons to allow the visitor to start and stop the countdown.

4. When the visitor clicks the Start Clock button, the startClock() function is called.

5. The startClock() function uses the window.prompt() method to gather the visitor's birthdate and planned retirement age.

6. The firstdate Date object from step 2 is filled with the visitor's birthdate. The variable retirementyear is then filled with the sum of the visitor's birthyear and the planned retirement age. Finally, the lastdate Date object from step 2 is filled with the visitor's date of retirement as calculated from the birthdate.

7. The last line of the startClock() function invokes the setInterval() method to call the showTime() function repeatedly each second. The ID for this task is stored in timerID.

8. The showTime() function creates the variable now as an instance of the Date object.

9. A variable called seconds is then filled with the number of seconds between the current moment and the moment the visitor retires. The getTime() method of the Date object returns the number of milliseconds between January 1, 1970, and whatever instance of the date object is invoking the method. Because the Date object lasttime represents a date in the future, the number of milliseconds returned by the getTime() method will be larger than the number returned when the now Date object invokes the getTime() method. By dividing the difference by 1000, we get the number of seconds between the two dates.

10. The various fields in the `clock` form are filled with calculated values based on the variable `seconds`. For example, the `minutesface` field will contain the number of minutes, which is equal to the seconds divided by 60. The `workdays` field value is calculated by multiplying the number of days by 0.65 because approximately 65% of the remaining days until retirement will be spent working.

11. A variable called `birthdatedisplay` is created to hold the formatted text string containing the visitor's birthdate. A variable called `retirementdisplay` is created to hold the formatted text string containing the visitor's retirement date. The strings are created using the technique explained in Listing 6.4.

12. The values in the text fields `birthdate` and `retirementdate` are then changed to the values in the variables `birthdatedisplay` and `retirementdate`.

☆ Summary

▷ JavaScript contains a set of core objects, including the Date object, that exist independently of any host environment such as a Web browser. To use the Date object, you first create an instance of it and then apply a method to obtain date and time information.

▷ A quick way to create a simple clock is to use the toLocaleString() method of the Date object, which returns the date and time formatted as text.

▷ To create customized presentations of the time, you obtain the current hour, minute, and seconds using methods of the Date object. These values can be stored as variables and then concatenated (joined together) to create a string of text to express the time.

▷ It is possible to vary the information displayed on your Web page according to the time or date. If code exists in the HEAD to test for the time of day, you can create variable content in the BODY using the document.write() method.

▷ JavaScript's Math object is a built-in calculator. To perform math operations on information obtained from text fields, you first convert the values to numbers using the parseInt() or parseFloat() function.

☆ Online References

Netscape has a complete reference for JavaScript 1.5 on its developer Web site. The section in Chapter One on the Date object has complete documentation.
`http://developer.netscape.com/docs/manuals/js/core/jsref15/ ¬ contents.html`

W3Schools.com offers tutorials and code samples to help you learn about using dates and times in JavaScript.
`http://www.w3schools.com/js/js_datetime.asp`

Earthweb offers a nice set of Time/Date samples and templates.
`http://webdeveloper.earthweb.com/pagedev/webjs/jstimedate`

☆ Review Questions

1. What is a host environment?
2. What date is used as the basis for all dates and times in JavaScript?
3. What value is returned by the getTime() method of the Date object?
4. Name three methods of the Date object that return zero-based data.

5. Which method of the Date object returns the date and time formatted as a text string to local standards?

6. What are the differences between the setInterval() and setTimeout() methods?

7. Do JavaScript statements contained in a function in the HEAD automatically execute when the page loads?

8. When is it possible to include scripts in the BODY?

9. If now.getDay() returns the number 6, to what day of the week does it refer?

10. If now.getMonth() returns the number 8, to what month does it refer?

☆ Hands-On Exercises

1. Create a Web page with a customized clock to display the date and time in whatever form you choose.

2. Create a page that greets your visitor with a time-appropriate message.

3. Create a page to give your visitor a horoscope.

4. Create a page to count the seconds, minutes, hours, days, and years until some important event occurs. Choose any event you like.

5. Create a page containing an e-mail form (see Chapter Three). In one of the fields of the form, continually update the number of seconds the visitor has spent viewing the form. After the form is submitted, the recipient of the e-mail will know how long it took the visitor to fill out the form.

CHAPTER SEVEN

COOKIES:
MAINTAINING STATE

Normally, the information visitors type into a form on a Web page gets transmitted to an e-mail address or database and is not available to other Web pages. Many times in Web development, however, it's convenient to retain this kind of information. If your site requires visitors to register with a name and password, for example, it would be convenient if the visitor's browser could remember the login information on subsequent visits. Another classic example is the shopping cart. Visitors click buttons to add products to their carts. Then they click a button to view the cart and checkout. The products they chose appear in a table on a new page together with a calculated amount due. In these examples, information entered on one page is retained on the visitor's computer and transferred to other pages or sent back to the server that created the page. This is known as **maintaining state** because the state of information on a page is maintained even after the page is no longer active. Maintaining state is often accomplished today with JavaScript and small pieces of information called **cookies**.

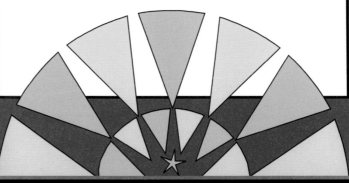

◎◎ Chapter Objectives

☆ To understand the nature and limitations of cookies

☆ To discover how to create and delete cookies

☆ To learn how to set and retrieve your visitors' preferences in cookies

☆ To understand how to customize your Web page using cookies

☆ To learn how to create a simple online shopping cart with cookies

◎◎ What Are Cookies?

In the parlance of the Internet, there are servers and clients. **Servers** are computers that store and transmit Web pages. **Clients** are the computers that receive and display these pages. A Web browser is often referred to as **client software**.

Suppose you're managing a Web site with a members-only section. A page sent by a server may contain a login form that appears on the client. The visitor using the client software (the browser) fills out the form with a name and password. The information is then sent back to the server for storage in a database. Each time the visitor returns to your page, he must remember his user name and password to log in again.

Now imagine that the visitor could click a button on your login screen to store the user name and password conveniently on his hard drive. Now each time he returns to your login page, the client software automatically retrieves the name and password and sends it to the server. The visitor's hard drive stores the login information until it's needed.

Cookie is a computer science term that refers to a piece of data held by an intermediary. In this case, the visitor's hard drive is the intermediary positioned between the client and the server. Cookies are actually small chunks of text usually stored in a plain old text file on the hard drive of the client. In the early 1990s, Lou Montulli created the original cookie specification for Netscape Navigator version 1.0, the first browser to have this feature.

Most major Web sites use cookies to personalize the browsing experience for each visitor. A customized start page is a common example. Yahoo, Excite, Netscape, and many others allow visitors to create such pages. These pages allow you to set preferences and then display, for example, your local weather, links to your favorite sites, even a table showing your stock portfolio. The first time you access your new start page, you type a user name and password. Each subsequent time you visit, however, no login is necessary because a cookie on your hard drive contains the login information. The client software matches the site address of the page with the site address stored in the cookie. If they match, the client software transmits the cookie containing the login information to the server.

⊚⊚ Frequently Asked Questions about Cookies

Q. Can cookies transmit computer viruses?

A. No. Viruses are computer programs. Plain text files are not computer programs. Because cookies are plain text residing in text files, they can't store or run computer programs the way viruses can. Also, the size of a cookie is limited to 4 kilobytes. Even if a computer program could be stored in a cookie, it would be difficult to create one that small.

Q. Can hackers use cookies to steal credit card information?

A. It's unlikely. Cookies contain only information that you supply. When you supply your credit card number during an online purchase, the Web server stores that information in its secure database and not in a cookie on your hard drive. Any company foolish enough to store sensitive information in a cookie would soon be out of business. Because cookies are readable text files, it would be only a matter of hours before some alert visitor noticed the presence of her credit card number in a cookie on her hard drive.

Q. Can hackers read the information stored in my cookies?

A. No. Cookies contain information about the site that created them. Only the site that creates a cookie can read that cookie. If some site actually stored sensitive information in a cookie, it would be the only site that could retrieve it.

Q. Can marketing firms invade my privacy using cookies?

A. Potentially. The DoubleClick Network stores customer profiles in cookies but does not store user names, e-mail addresses, or telephone numbers. Instead, each customer profile is anonymous. Banner ads on sites that use the DoubleClick service are customized to suit the interests of the person described in the customer profile. In February 2000, DoubleClick proposed to link these customer profiles with actual identities. The furor that arose was enough to convince DoubleClick and other companies that such behavior would yield nothing but ill will. Even so, many persons feel uncomfortable with the idea that they are being profiled on the Internet.

Q. Is there anything I can do to minimize privacy issues with cookies?

A. Certainly. All Web browsers have preference settings to allow you to manage your cookies. You can choose to have the browser automatically accept all cookies, never accept any cookies, or ask you each time a site wishes to send a cookie. Also, sites that use cookies to store visitor preferences should have a posted policy on what information is stored and how it will be used.

Q. How many cookies can I create for my Web page?

A. No more than 20 cookie records can be stored in the cookie property per domain. Most professional sites that use cookies store only one cookie to identify the visitor with a unique ID number or text string. The rest of the data needed to customize the visitor's experience is stored in a related database record on the server. This is a good practice because it avoids storing sensitive information in cookie records.

◎◎ Creating and Deleting Cookies

The cookie is a property of the document object. The value of the `cookie` property consists of a string of text. In most cases, creating a cookie involves creating only a cookie name and its associated value. In this example, the `cookie` property is set to contain a cookie called `username` with a value of `clara`:

```
document.cookie = "username=clara";
```

Optional information in the cookie can specify when it expires. After the expiration date, the browser automatically deletes the cookie. If an expiration date is not specified, the cookie expires when the visitor exits or quits the Web browser.

```
document.cookie = "username=clara; ¬
expires=Mon, 18-Jun-01 00:00:01 GMT";
```

The expiration date is always expressed in **GMT (Greenwich Mean Time)**. To convert local time to GMT, you could use a sequence of statements like the snippet shown next. This sequence creates an expiration date one year in the future by finding the number of milliseconds elapsed since January 1, 1970 (the `getTime()` method), and adding a year's worth of milliseconds ($365*24*60*60*1000$). The `toGMTString()` method converts the new date to GMT.

```
var expirationdate = new Date();
var oneyear = ¬
expirationdate.getTime() + (365 * 24 * 60 * 60 * 1000);
expirationdate.setTime(oneyear);
document.cookie = "username=clara; ¬
expires= " + expirationdate.toGMTString();
```

Path and domain information are sometimes added to a cookie to specify the location of pages that are authorized to retrieve the cookie. If these options are not set, the location and domain of the page creating the cookie are assumed.

```
document.cookie = "username=clara; ¬
expires=Mon, 18-Jun-01 00:00:01 GMT; ¬
path=/aw; domain=stevenestrella.com";
```

Finally, you may require that the server be using a secure channel (the HTTPS protocol) before sending the cookie.

```
document.cookie = "username=clara; ¬
expires=Mon, 18-Jun-01 00:00:01 GMT; ¬
path=/aw; domain=stevenestrella.com; secure";
```

The browser stores the cookie as plain text. The exact appearance of the cookie will vary among browsers. The following cookie records come from the cookie text file of Netscape Communicator 4.7. They were created by a page located in the `/aw` directory on `www.stevenestrella.com`. Neither the expiration date nor the secure option was set, and that's why the word `FALSE` appears twice in each cookie record.

```
www.stevenestrella.com  FALSE  /
   aw   FALSE  992919409  username      clara
www.stevenestrella.com  FALSE  /
   aw   FALSE  992919409  colorchoice  aqua
```

Any Web page located in the /aw directory of www.stevenestrella.com can retrieve the information in these records. Such a page could then greet the visitor with "Hello Clara!" and set the background color to aqua automatically.

Bill Dortch of hIdaho designs created a set of functions in the mid-1990s to assist Web developers in creating, reading, and deleting cookies. Mr. Dortch has generously placed these routines in the public domain. The code in Listing 7.1 is based on the Dortch code with some cosmetic modifications to make it easier to read and understand.

☆ **SHORTCUT**   To save time later, place all of Listing 7.1 in your mylibrary.js file.

```
/* Cookie Code based on code by Bill Dortch of hIdaho
designs. */
function SetCookie(name,value,expires,path,domain, ¬
secure){
    var temp = name + "=" + escape(value);
    if (expires){
        temp += "; expires=" + expires.toGMTString();
    }
    if (path){
        temp += "; path=" + path;
    }
    if (domain){
        temp += "; domain=" + domain;
    }
    if (secure){
        temp += "; secure";
    }
    document.cookie = temp;
}
function GetCookie(name){
    var arg = name + "=";
    var alen = arg.length;
    var clen = document.cookie.length;
    var i = 0;
    while (i < clen) {
        var j = i + alen;
        if (document.cookie.substring(i,j) == arg){
            return getCookieVal(j);
        }
        i = document.cookie.indexOf(" ", i) + 1;
        if (i == 0) break;
    }
    return null;
}
```

```
function getCookieVal(offset){
    var endstr = document.cookie.indexOf(";", offset);
    if (endstr == -1){
        endstr = document.cookie.length;
    }
    return unescape(document.cookie.substring(offset, ¬
endstr));
}
function DeleteCookie (name,path,domain) {
    if (GetCookie(name)) {
        var temp = name + "=";
        temp += ((path) ? "; path=" + path : "");
        temp += ((domain) ? "; domain=" + domain : "");
        temp += "; expires=Thu, 01-Jan-70 00:00:01 GMT";
        document.cookie = temp;
    }
}
/* End of Cookie Code */
```

> DeleteCookie()
> eliminates a cookie by
> setting its expiration
> date to a date in the
> past.

Listing 7.1 Public Domain Cookie Code by Bill Dortch

☆ **WARNING** A Dangerous Loop

Listing 7.1 contains a **while loop** structure in the GetCookie() function. Here's the form of the while loop:

```
while (condition is true){
    statements go here;
}
```

The condition remains true until one of the statements in the loop changes it to false. With the GetCookie() function, an index variable i is set to 0 before the loop begins. The loop ends when a value is returned or the break statement is executed. Loops that use the while structure are a bit more dangerous for beginning programmers. Be careful when using the while loop structure to avoid creating endless loops that may freeze up your computer.

How Does It Work?

1. The SetCookie() function receives as many as five parameters. Only the name and value parameters are required. A temporary variable temp is created to hold the name of the cookie and the value. The escape() function converts any nonalphanumeric characters to their hexadecimal equivalents. For example, if the value is a name with a space in it, such as Bob Fitch, the escape() function returns Bob%20Fitch, with the hexadecimal %20 representing the space. The function then uses conditional structures to determine whether any of the optional parameters are present and adds their values to the variable temp. The contents of temp are then assigned to the cookie property of the document object.

2. The GetCookie function receives only one parameter, the name of the cookie. It then adds the = to the name and stores it in a new variable arg. The

length of `arg` is stored in another variable, `alen`, and the length of the cookie is stored in `clen`. Then a loop begins with the variable `i` set to 0. The form of this loop is a little different from the for loop structure you learned in Chapter Two. The while loop structure continues as long as the condition is true. In this case, the condition is that the value in `i` continues to be less than the value in `clen`. The loop examines substrings of the cookie to find a match for the cookie name. When a match is found, the function makes note of the number of the character where the value begins (represented by `j`). This **offset** number is passed to the `getCookieVal()` function to extract the value by looking at the entire cookie string beginning at the offset character.

3. The `getCookieVal()` function creates a variable `endstr` to hold the character number of the last character in the requested value. It does this by using the `indexOf()` method to locate the first occurrence of a semicolon after the character number represented by the offset parameter. If there is no semicolon, the value that begins at the offset is the last one in the cookie. In that case, the `indexOf()` method returns a value of –1, and `endstr` is set to match the length of the cookie. Finally, the substring of the cookie that begins at the offset and ends at `endstr` is passed to the `unescape()` function. The `unescape()` function converts any hexadecimal characters such as `%20` back into readable text. `Bob%20Fitch` returns as `Bob Fitch`.

4. The `DeleteCookie()` function is similar to the `SetCookie()` function. The `DeleteCookie()` function sets the expiration date to one second after midnight of January 1, 1970. This is the beginning of Internet time. Each time the browser starts up, it deletes all expired cookies. Setting the expiration date to a date in the past is the standard way to delete a cookie.

◎◎ Setting and Getting Your First Cookie

Now that you have added Listing 7.1 to `mylibrary.js`, it's time to make your first cookie. Listing 7.2 is a simple page with text fields for your visitor to enter his name and favorite color. The visitor can then store his information in cookies by clicking the Make Cookies button. The next time he loads the page, the information is retrieved from the cookie and displayed in the two bottom fields on the page.

```
<html><head><title>Cookie Factory</title>
<script type="text/javascript" language="JavaScript"
src="mylibrary.js">
</script>
<script type="text/javascript" language="JavaScript">
<!--
function showCookies(){
    if (GetCookie("visitor") || ¬
GetCookie("colorchoice")){
```

This page will not work unless you have placed Bill Dortch's cookie code in `mylibrary.js`.

```
        document.cookieform.visitorcookie.value = ¬
GetCookie("visitor");
        document.cookieform.colorcookie.value = ¬
GetCookie("colorchoice");
    }else{
        document.cookieform.visitorcookie.value = ¬
"No visitor cookie found.";
        document.cookieform.colorcookie.value = ¬
"No color cookie found.";
    }
}
function makeCookies(){
    var visitorname = document.cookieform.visitor.value;
    var visitorcolor = document.cookieform.color.value
    SetCookie("visitor",visitorname);
    SetCookie("colorchoice",visitorcolor);
    alert("Two cookies have been created.");
}
//-->
</script>
</head>
<body bgcolor="white" onload="showCookies();">
<h1>Your First Cookie</h1>
<form name="cookieform">
<p><input type="text" name="visitor" size="35" value=
"Type your name here."></p>
<p><input type="text" name="color" size="35" value=
"Type your favorite color here."></p>
<ol>
<li>Click this button to make your cookies.<br>
<input type="button" value="Make Cookies" onclick=
"makeCookies();"></li>
<li>Go to any other page on the internet.</li>
<li>Click the back button to return to this page and see
your cookies.</li>
</ol>
<br><br>
<hr>
<p>Cookies will appear here.</p>
<p><input type="text" name="visitorcookie" size="35"
value="">
<input type="text" name="colorcookie" size="20"
value=""></p>
</form>
</body>
</html>
```

Listing 7.2 A Simple Page to Set Two Cookies

Figure 7.1 shows the output of Listing 7.2.

Figure 7.1 Output of Listing 7.2 Showing Retrieved Cookies

How Does It Work?

1. The `mylibrary.js` file is loaded into memory when the HEAD loads. When the page finishes loading, an `onload` handler in the BODY tag calls the `showCookies()` function. The `showCookies()` function calls the `GetCookie()` function to see whether the cookies `visitor` and `colorchoice` exist. If either of these cookies exists, the `showCookies()` function displays the cookie values in the `visitorcookie` and `colorcookie` fields.

2. The visitor types a name and color choice and clicks the Make Cookies button.

3. The `makeCookies()` function places the values the visitor typed into two variables: `visitorname` and `visitorcolor`.

4. The `SetCookie()` function, stored in `mylibrary.js`, is called with the word `visitor` as the cookie name and the variable `visitorname` as the cookie value.

5. The `SetCookie()` function, stored in `mylibrary.js`, is called with the word `colorchoice` as the cookie name and the variable `visitorcolor` as the cookie value.

6. An alert notifies the visitor that his cookies have been created.

7. The visitor browses any other page on the Web and then returns to this page.

8. The `onload` handler calls the `showCookies()` function and retrieves and displays the information found in the cookies.

◎◎ Customizing a Web Page with Cookies

Now that you have built a simple page to set and get cookies, you can build a slightly more elaborate page. Listing 7.3 builds a page that automatically sets the background color to the visitor's preferred color and displays a welcome message that includes the date the visitor last visited the page.

```
<html><head><title>Cookie Factory</title>
<script type="text/javascript" language="JavaScript"
src="mylibrary.js">
</script>
<script type="text/javascript" language="JavaScript">
<!--
function showCookies(){
    var thelastvisit = GetCookie("lastvisited");
    if (thelastvisit){
        var thevisitor = GetCookie("visitor");
        var thecolor = GetCookie("colorchoice");
        showSelectValue("cookieform","colorpicker", ¬
thecolor);
        var thewelcome = "Welcome back, " + thevisitor ¬
+ ".";
        thewelcome += "Your last visit was:\n" ¬
+ thelastvisit + ".";
        var thefeedback = "visitor=" + thevisitor + "; ";
        thefeedback += "colorchoice=" + thecolor + ";\n";
        thefeedback += "lastvisited=" + thelastvisit;
        document.cookieform.cookiejar.value = thefeedback;
        document.cookieform.visitor.value = thewelcome;
        setBG();
    }else{
        document.cookieform.cookiejar.value = ¬
"No cookies found."
    }
}
function makeCookies(){
    var now = new Date();
    var lastvisit = now.toLocaleString();
    var expHours = 24;
    var expireDate = new Date();
    expireDate.setTime(expireDate.getTime() + (expHours ¬
* 60 * 60 * 1000));
    var visitorname = document.cookieform.visitor.value;
    var visitorcolor = getSelectValue("cookieform", ¬
"colorpicker");
    SetCookie("lastvisited",lastvisit,expireDate);
```

The setBG() function changes the background color to the color chosen on the visitor's Web site.

```
      SetCookie("visitor",visitorname,expireDate);
      SetCookie("colorchoice",visitorcolor,expireDate);
      alert("Go away and come back to this page to see ¬
the results.");
}
function trashCookies(){
      DeleteCookie("lastvisited");
      DeleteCookie("visitor");
      DeleteCookie("colorchoice");
      alert("All cookies have been deleted.");
      showSelectValue("cookieform","colorpicker","none");
      document.bgColor = "white";
      document.cookieform.visitor.value = "Type your ¬
name here.";
      document.cookieform.cookiejar.value = "No cookies ¬
found.";
}
function setBG(){
      document.bgColor = getSelectValue("cookieform", ¬
"colorpicker");
}
//-->
</script>
</head>
<body bgcolor="white" onload="showCookies();">
<form name="cookieform">
<h1 align="center">Cookie Factory</h1>
<table border="0" align="center">
<tr>
<td align="center" valign="top">
<img src="images/cookies.gif" alt="cookies" name=
"cookiepict" width="135" height="135" align="left"></td>
<td align="left" valign="top">
<p><b>Your Name:</b><br>
<textarea name="visitor" rows="3" cols="60" value="">
Type your name here.</textarea></p>
<p><b>A Background Color:</b> <select name="colorpicker"
onchange="setBG();">
<option selected value="none">Select a Color</option>
<option value="aqua">aqua</option>
<option value="fuchsia">fuchsia</option>
<option value="lime">lime</option>
<option value="teal">teal</option>
<option value="white">white</option>
<option value="yellow">yellow</option>
</select></p>
```

```
<p><input type="button" value="Make Cookies"
onclick="makeCookies();">
<input type="button" value="Delete Cookies"
onclick="trashCookies();"></p>
<p><b>Your cookies:</b><br>
<textarea name="cookiejar" rows="3" cols="60"
value=""></textarea></p>
</td>
</tr>
</table>
</form>
</body>
</html>
```

Listing 7.3 Customized Web Page with Cookies

☆ **SHORTCUT**   **Using the `mylibrary.js` File**

In Listing 7.3 the `getSelectValue()` and `showSelectValue()` functions are called but not defined in the code. Instead, they're stored in the `mylibrary.js` file. These two functions were created in Chapter Three. By continuing to add functions to `mylibrary.js` you will be able to more quickly create new pages without having to reinvent the wheel each time you perform a familiar task.

Figure 7.2 shows the output of Listing 7.3.

Figure 7.2 Output of Listing 7.3 Showing Retrieved Cookies

How Does It Work?

1. The `mylibrary.js` file is loaded into memory when the HEAD loads. When the page finishes loading, an `onload` handler in the BODY tag calls the `showCookies()` function. The `showCookies()` function calls the `GetCookie()` function to attempt to retrieve the `lastvisited` cookie containing the date of the visitor's last visit. The result is stored in a variable called `thelastvisit`. If `thelastvisit` is empty, the string No cookies found. is displayed in the `cookiejar` field on `cookieform`. If `thelastvisit` contains anything at all, the remaining `visitor` and `colorchoice` cookies are also retrieved. These cookie values are stored in the variables `thevisitor` and `thecolor`.

2. The `showSelectValue()` function (from Chapter Three) stored in the `mylibrary.js` file changes the display of the `colorpicker` SELECT to match the visitor's preferred color.

3. A new variable, `thewelcome`, is created to hold the welcome message. It is filled with a concatenated text string containing the visitor's name and the date she last visited.

4. A new variable, `thefeedback`, is created to hold a text string to show the format of the cookie. It is filled with a concatenated text string containing each name-value pair from the cookie.

5. The contents of `thefeedback` are displayed in the `cookiejar` field on the `cookieform`.

6. The contents of `thewelcome` are displayed in the `visitor` field on the `cookieform`.

7. The `setBG()` function is called. The `setBG()` function calls the `getSelectValue()` function (from Chapter Three) to get the selected value from the `colorpicker` SELECT. Then the `bgColor` property of the `document` object is changed to the selected background color.

8. The visitor chooses a new background color using the `colorpicker` SELECT. The `onchange` handler in the SELECT calls the `setBG()` function to change the background color immediately.

9. The visitor changes the name in the `visitor` field and then clicks the Make Cookies button. An `onclick` handler in the button calls the `makeCookies()` function.

10. The `makeCookies()` function creates a new Date object to establish the current date as the date the visitor last visited the page. The date is stored in the variable `lastvisit` as a text string in the local format using the `toLocaleString()` method of the `date` object.

11. A variable, `expHours`, is created to hold the number of hours before the cookie will expire. A second Date object, `expireDate`, is created and filled with a new time 24 hours in the future.

12. Two new variables—`visitorname` and `visitorcolor`—are filled with the values the visitor entered in the `visitor` field and the `colorpicker` `SELECT`.

13. The `SetCookie()` function is called three times to create the cookies `lastvisited`, `visitor`, and `colorchoice` with the values found in the variables `lastvisit`, `visitorname`, and `visitorcolor` and set to expire in 24 hours.

14. An alert notifies the visitor that the cookies are finished.

15. The visitor goes to another Web page and then returns to this page. When she returns, the `onload` handler in the `BODY` tag calls the `showCookies()` function to display the appropriate welcome message and change the background color to reflect the visitor's preference.

16. The visitor clicks the Delete Cookies Button. The `trashCookies()` function is called.

17. The `trashCookies()` function calls the `DeleteCookie()` function three times to delete the three cookies. An alert informs the visitor that the cookies have been deleted. The `SELECT` is reset. The background color is set to white. Default values are set for the `visitor` and `cookiejar` fields.

◎◎ Creating a Simple Shopping Cart

The most basic shopping cart for an online store involves three pages. The first page displays the products along with buttons so that the visitor can add the products to his shopping cart. The second page displays the contents of the cart and calculates an amount due. The third page displays a form for the visitor to fill out with address and credit card information. In the next two examples you will create the first two pages to learn how cookies are used in shopping cart applications.

> ☆**TIP**   You can adapt this example for any project in which you wish to store visitor input in a cookie. Online surveys or self-grading tests are two examples.

Listing 7.4 creates the first page. In this sample store, you will sell flags of Canada, the United States, and the United Kingdom.

```
<html><head><title>Flag Store</title>
<script type="text/javascript" language="JavaScript"
src="mylibrary.js">
</script>
<script type="text/javascript" language="JavaScript">
<!--
var myproducts = new Array("canada","usa","uk");
var itemqty = 0;
function showCookies(){
    for (i=0;i<myproducts.length;i++){
        var qtyWanted = GetCookie(myproducts[i]);
```

```
        itemqty = qtyWanted ? qtyWanted : "0";
        document.flagform[myproducts[i]+"qty"].value = ¬
itemqty;
    }
}
function addToCart(country){
    itemqty = document.flagform[country + "qty"].value;
    itemqty = parseInt(itemqty);
    SetCookie(country,itemqty);
    var feedback = "An order for " + itemqty + ¬
" flag(s) of ";
    feedback += country.toUpperCase();
    feedback += " has been added to your shopping cart.";
    feedback += " Please click 'Check Out' when ¬
finished."
    alert(feedback);
}
function checkOut(){
    window.location.href = "listing7.5.html";
}
//-->
</script>
</head>
<body bgcolor="white" onload="showCookies();">
<form name="flagform">
<h1 align="center">Flag Store</h1>
<table border="0" align="center">
<tr>
<td align="center">
<img src="images/canada.gif" name="canadaflag"
width="135" height="104">
<h4>Canada</h4>
</td>
<td align="center">
<p><b>Quantity:</b><br>
<input type="TEXT" name="canadaqty" size="5"
value="0"><br>
<b>$45 each</b></p>
</td>
<td align="center">
<p><input type="button" value="Add to Cart"
onclick="addToCart('canada');">
</p>
</td>
</tr>
<tr>
<td align="center">
```

```
<img src="images/usa.gif" name="usaflag" width="135"
height="104">
<h4>The United States</h4>
</td>
<td align="center">
<p><b>Quantity:</b><br>
<input type="TEXT" name="usaqty" size="5" value="0"><br>
<b>$35 each</b></p>
</td>
<td align="center">
<p><input type="button" value="Add to Cart"
onclick="addToCart('usa');">
</p>
</td>
</tr>
<tr>
<td align="center">
<img src="images/uk.gif" name="ukflag" width="135"
height="104">
<h4>The United Kingdom</h4>
</td>
<td align="center">
<p><b>Quantity:</b><br>
<input type="TEXT" name="ukqty" size="5" value="0"><br>
<b>$40 each</b></p>
</td>
<td align="center">
<p><input type="button" value="Add to Cart"
onclick="addToCart('uk');">
</p>
</td>
</tr>
</table>
<div align="center">
<p><input type="button" value="CHECK OUT"
onclick="checkOut();">
</p>
</div>
</form>
</body>
</html>
```

Listing 7.4 Storefront for a Cookie-Based Shopping Cart

Figure 7.3 shows the output of Listing 7.4.

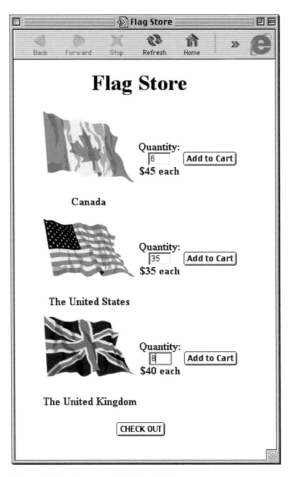

Figure 7.3 Output of Listing 7.4

How Does It Work?

1. The HEAD portion of the document loads the mylibrary.js file containing all the Dortch cookie code. Then a new array is created called myproducts to hold the names of the three flags you're selling. The remaining functions load into memory.

2. The BODY loads a table displaying the flags. A FORM contains text fields for visitors to indicate the quantity desired of each flag and buttons to add each item to the shopping cart. The onload handler in the BODY tag calls the showCookies() function to find any cookies that might exist if the visitor has shopped here before. The showCookies() function uses a loop to check for cookies that correspond to the names found in the myproducts array. Any values it finds are displayed in the appropriate form field.

3. The visitor makes changes to the quantity fields and clicks each Add to Cart button. An `onclick` handler in the button calls the `addToCart()` function and passes a parameter containing the name of the flag's country.

4. The `addToCart()` function finds the value in a field whose name is the combination of the name of the country and the characters `qty`. That value is placed in the variable `itemqty`, and then converted to an integer with the `parseInt()` function.

5. The `SetCookie()` function is called to create a cookie with the name set to the content of the variable `country` and the value set to the content of the variable `itemqty`.

6. A variable called `feedback` is created to hold a string of text to inform the user that his order has been added to the shopping cart.

7. The visitor clicks the Check Out button. The `checkOut()` function is called, and the browser loads the page called `listing7.5.html`.

Listing 7.5 creates the second page, where the visitor reviews the items in the shopping cart before proceeding with payment.

```
<html><head><title>Flag Store Shopping Cart</title>
<script type="text/javascript" language="JavaScript"
src="mylibrary.js">
</script>
<script type="text/javascript" language="JavaScript">
<!--
var myproducts = new Array("canada","usa","uk");
var myprices = new Array("45","35","40");
var itemqty = 0;
function showCookies(){
    for (i=0;i<myproducts.length;i++){
        var qtyWanted = GetCookie(myproducts[i]);
        itemqty = qtyWanted ? qtyWanted : "0";
        itemqty = parseInt(itemqty);
        document.flagform[myproducts[i]+"qty"].value = ¬
itemqty;
    }
    calculate();
}
function trashCookies(){
    for (i=0;i<myproducts.length;i++){
        DeleteCookie(myproducts[i]);
        document.flagform[myproducts[i]+"qty"].value = ¬
"0";
    }
    calculate();
}
```

```
function calculate(){
    var amountdue=0;
    for (i=0;i<myproducts.length;i++){
        itemqty = ¬
document.flagform[myproducts[i]+"qty"].value
        var itemtotal = parseInt(itemqty) * myprices[i];
        document.flagform[myproducts[i]+"total"].value = ¬
itemtotal;
        amountdue += parseInt(itemtotal);
        document.flagform["grandtotal"].value = amountdue;
    }
}
function qtyUpdate(){
    for (i=0;i<myproducts.length;i++){
        itemqty = document.flagform[myproducts[i] + ¬
"qty"].value;
        itemqty = parseInt(itemqty);
        SetCookie(myproducts[i],itemqty);
    }
    calculate();
}
function goStore(){
    window.location.href = "listing7.4.html";
}
//-->
</script>
</head>
<body bgcolor="white" onload="showCookies();">
<div align="center">
<h1>Your Shopping Cart</h1>
<form name="flagform">
<table width="450" border="1" cellspacing="2"
cellpadding="2">
<tr>
<td width="250"><b>PRODUCT</b></td>
<td width="50"><b>QTY</b></td>
<td width="50"><b>PRICE</b></td>
<td width="100"><b>TOTALS</b></td>
</tr>
<tr>
<td><b>FLAG OF CANADA</b></td>
<td><input type="text" name="canadaqty" size="5"
onchange="qtyUpdate();" value="0"> </td>
<td>$45</td>
<td>$ <input type="text" name="canadatotal" size="10"
onchange="qtyUpdate();" value="0"> </td>
```

The `calculate()` function is called by most of the other functions in this script.

```
</tr>
<tr>
<td><b>FLAG OF THE UNITED STATES</b></td>
<td><input type="text" name="usaqty" size="5" onchange=
"qtyUpdate();" value="0"> </td>
<td>$35</td>
<td>$ <input type="text" name="usatotal" size="10"
onchange="qtyUpdate();" value="0"> </td>
</tr>
<tr>
<td><b>FLAG OF THE UNITED KINGDOM</b></td>
<td><input type="text" name="ukqty" size="5" onchange=
"qtyUpdate();" value="0"> </td>
<td>$40</td>
<td>$ <input type="text" name="uktotal" size="10"
onchange="qtyUpdate();" value="0"> </td>
</tr>
<tr>
<td colspan="3" align="right">AMOUNT DUE</td>
<td>$ <input type="text" name="grandtotal" size="10"
onchange="qtyUpdate();" value="0"> </td>
</tr>
</table>
<p>
<input type="button" value="RETURN TO STORE"
onclick="goStore();"> <input type="button" value="CLEAR
FORM" onclick="trashCookies();">
<input type="button" value="PROCEED TO PAYMENT"
onclick="window.alert('This simulation ends here.');">
</p>
</form>
</div>
</body>
</html>
```

Listing 7.5 Order Form for a Cookie-Based Shopping Cart

Figure 7.4 shows the output of Listing 7.5.

How Does It Work?

1. The HEAD portion of the document loads the mylibrary.js file containing all the Dortch cookie code. Then a new array is created called myproducts to hold the names of the three flags you're selling. Another array is created called myprices to hold the prices of the flags. The remaining functions load into memory.

Figure 7.4 Output of Listing 7.5 Showing Calculated Amount Due

2. The BODY loads a table having a row for each product and a final row for the amount due. There are four columns for product, quantity, price, and totals. A FORM contains text fields in the second column to display the quantity desired of each flag. The prices in the third column are already set so they appear as plain text. The totals in the fourth column are calculated from the quantities in the second column.

3. The onload handler in the BODY tag calls the showCookies() function to find the cookies the visitor created while shopping at the previous page. The showCookies() function uses a loop to check for cookies that correspond to the names found in the myproducts array. Any values it finds are displayed in the appropriate form field.

4. The calculate() function is called as the last statement in the showCookies() function. A variable called amountdue is created. Then a loop steps through the elements of the myproducts array. The first statement inside the loop finds the value in a field whose name is the combination of the name of the country and the characters qty. That value is placed in the variable itemqty. The parseInt() function then converts the content of itemqty to an integer, and that value is multiplied by the price of the item found in the myprices array. The result is stored in a variable called itemtotal and then displayed in a field whose name is the combination of the current element of the myproducts array (canada, usa, or uk) and the word total. The variable amountdue is then increased by the amount stored in itemtotal and displayed in the field grandtotal.

5. The visitor makes any desired changes to the quantity fields. An onchange handler in each field calls the qtyUpdate() function. The qtyUpdate() function updates the three cookies and calls the calculate() function to update the item totals and the amount due.

6. The visitor decides to examine the product photos on the Flag Store page again before proceeding. He clicks the Return to Store button, which calls the `goStore()` function and loads the page called `listing7.4.html`.

7. The Flag Store page from Listing 7.4 loads into the browser window. When the loading is complete, an onload handler in the BODY tag retrieves and displays the updated quantities for each item from the cookies.

☆**TIP**   **Becoming an Internet Mogul**

Online payment systems such as PayPal.com allow small businesses and individuals to sell products from their Web sites without having to set up costly credit card processing and merchant banking accounts. PayPal takes care of all the credit card processing and retains a small portion of the payment as a fee. The remaining funds collected are then transferred to your checking account. Visit `http://www.ti-me.org` to see how a small nonprofit organization uses PayPal to accept membership payments online.

Creating a Simple Shopping Cart

☆ Summary

▷ Cookies are small pieces of information stored on the visitor's hard drive. Cookies are mostly harmless, but valid privacy concerns exist about the use of cookies in conjunction with invasive marketing techniques. You can create as many as 20 cookies per domain.

▷ Cookies are set when a JavaScript statement in a Web page assigns content to the cookie property of the document object. By default, the content includes information about the domain and directory location of the page that created it. When a Web page attempts to retrieve a cookie, the location of the Web page is compared to the domain and directory of the page that created the cookie. If the two locations do not match, the cookie cannot be retrieved. You can set an expiration date for your cookies. The form of the expiration date is always GMT. Bill Dortch's cookie code is widely used on the Internet and has been placed in the public domain.

▷ One popular use of cookies is to store visitor preferences, such as background color and login information.

▷ When a Web page retrieves information from a cookie, the page can act on that information by changing the page appearance to suit the expressed preferences of the visitor.

▷ Another popular use of cookies is to retain selected items as visitors move through the pages of an online shopping cart. The shopping cart technique can also be adapted to delivering surveys or tests online.

☆ Online References

Marshall Brain's How Stuff Works site has a nice article on cookies.
`http://www.howstuffworks.com/cookie.htm`

Webopedia's basic definition of cookies
`http://webopedia.internet.com/TERM/c/cookie.html`

CookieCentral.com offers an overview of cookies and links to related news articles.
`http://www.cookiecentral.com`

The Electronic Privacy Information Center offers information to address privacy concerns about cookies.
`http://www.epic.org/privacy/internet/cookies/`

Roger Clarke offers a scholarly article and basic history about cookies.
`http://www.anu.edu.au/people/Roger.Clarke/II/Cookies.html`

129

☆ Review Questions

1. What is the meaning of the computer science term *cookie*?
2. What is the difference between a client and a server?
3. Who created the original cookie specification?
4. What is client software?
5. Why can't cookies transmit computer viruses?
6. What prevents computer hackers from viewing information stored in cookies?
7. How does the `while` loop differ from the more familiar `for` loop?
8. What do the `escape()` and `unescape()` functions do?
9. What function is used to store the number values in a text field as integers?
10. Describe the standard method for deleting a cookie.

☆ Hands-On Exercises

1. Create a page on your site that allows visitors to store preferences for background color, name, and greeting.
2. Create a page on your site that uses `document.write()` to greet the visitor by name if the visitor's name is stored in a cookie. See Listing 6.3 for an example of using `document.write()` to display text created by a function in the HEAD.
3. Create a simple shopping cart to sell a product of your choice.
4. Create a multipage test in which each question is on a separate page but the cumulative score is stored in a cookie and displayed on each page of the test.
5. Modify Listing 7.5 to use `document.write()` to display the quantities and totals instead of using input text fields.

CHAPTER EIGHT

WORKING WITH WINDOWS AND FRAMES

Using multiple windows and frames in Web site design opens up a world of possibilities. That world expands even more when you apply scripting to these objects. With JavaScript, you can open new windows of any size and location. You can control the placement of your documents in your framesets and prevent their appearance in the framesets of others. You can also write content to new windows and frames dynamically.

◉◉ Chapter Objectives

☆ To open and close new windows of any size or position with JavaScript

☆ To write new content to the windows you create

☆ To prevent a web page from appearing in someone else's frameset

☆ To force a Web page to appear in your frameset

☆ To dynamically create content and place it in a frame

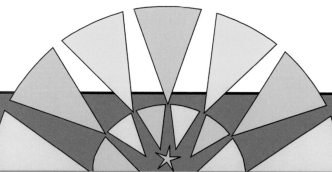

◉◉ Using Window Methods to Enhance the HTML Builder

In Chapter Two you learned how to create a Web page that assembles the basic HTML code for a page. Listing 8.1 expands on this idea, adding a button to display the assembled page in a new window. The code-testing feature from Listing 2.9 is added so that you can experiment with JavaScript commands.

```
<html><head><title>HTML Builder Page with Window
Generator</title>
<script type="text/javascript" language="Javascript"
src="mylibrary.js">
</script>

<script type="text/javascript" language="Javascript">
<!--
/* Make sure you place the following code in
mylibrary.js */
var myWindow = null;
function openWin(url,targetname,W,H,L,T,thefeatures) {
    var params = "";
    var nofeatures = "toolbar=0,location=0, ¬
directories=0,status=0,";
    nofeatures += "menubar=0,scrollbars=0,resizable=0, ¬
copyhistory=0";
    var basicfeatures = "scrollbars=1,resizable=1, ¬
menubar=1";
    var morefeatures = "toolbar=1,location=1, ¬
directories=1,";
    morefeatures += "status=1,copyhistory=1";
    var dimensions = "width=" + W + ",height=" + H;
    var placement = "left="  + L + ",top=" + T;
    placement += ",screenX="  + L + ",screenY=" + T;

    switch (thefeatures){
        case "none":
            params += nofeatures;
            break;
        case "basic":
            params += basicfeatures;
            break;
        case "full":
            params += basicfeatures + "," + morefeatures;
            break;
        default:
            params += thefeatures;
    }
```

The switch control structure makes decisions that depend on the value of a variable. In this case the value of the parameter variable thefeatures determines the value of the variable params.

The placement variable contains values for left/top and screenX/screenY. Use both to ensure compatibility with all browsers.

```
    /* Adds the dimensions and placement info to the
params variable. */
    params += "," + dimensions + "," + placement;
    /* The window.open() method creates myWindow. */
    myWindow = window.open(url,targetname,params);
}

function closeWin(){
    if (myWindow != null){
        myWindow.close();
        myWindow = null;
    }
}
/* End of openWin() and closeWin() functions for
mylibrary.js file */

function showPage(){
    var displaycode = document.pageform.mycode.value;
    openWin("","myPopup",400,200,100,40,"basic");
    myWindow.document.write(displaycode) ;
    myWindow.focus();
    myWindow.document.close() ;
}
function runCode(){
    var thecode = document.pageform.codefield.value;
    eval(thecode);
}
//-->
</script>
</head>
<body bgcolor="white">
<h1>HTML Builder with Window Generator</h1>
<p>Fill out the form below to create a basic HTML page.
</p>
<form name="pageform">
<h2>Title: <input type="text" name="pagetitle" size="50"
value="A Basic HTML Page"></h2>
<h2>Body Text:</h2>
<p><textarea name="bodytext" cols="80" rows="4">
Replace the text you are reading now with the text of
your choice.
</textarea></p>
<p><input type="button" value="Build My Page"
onclick="buildPage();"></p>
<h2>Code for you to copy will appear below.</h2>
<p><textarea name="mycode" cols="80" rows="8">
The code will be shown here.
```

```
</textarea></p>
<p><input type="button" name="ShowIt" value="Show My
Page" onclick="showPage();"> <input type="button"
name="CloseIt" value="Close New Window"
onclick="closeWin();"></p>
<h2>Experiment with JavaScript commands here.</h2>
<p><textarea name="codefield" cols="80" rows="6">
var displaycode = ¬
document.pageform.mycode.value;
openWin("","somename",400,200,100,40,"none");
myWindow.document.write(displaycode);
myWindow.focus();
myWindow.document.close();
</textarea></p>
<p><input type="button" name="RunIt" value="Execute my
code" onclick="runCode();"></p>
</form>
</body>
</html>
```

This text looks like JavaScript code but is not surrounded by the SCRIPT tag. Therefore, the browser interprets it as plain text.

When this button is clicked, the browser calls the runCode() function. The runCode() function calls the eval() function to take the text in the textarea above and execute it as JavaScript code.

Listing 8.1 The HTML Builder Page with Window Generator and Code Tester

To understand the script, you must first understand the open() method of the window object. This method opens a new window.

```
window.open(URL,targetname,features);
window.open("http://www.awl.com","aw","width=800, ¬
height=600,scrollbars=1");
```

The window.open() method takes three parameters. The first parameter, URL, contains the location of a document to load into the new window. The second parameter, targetname, contains a text string to identify the window to any links on your page that have a TARGET attribute. That allows you to build simple links in one window that change the content of the new window.

```
<a href="newpage.html" target="aw">link</A>
```

The third parameter, features, contains a comma-separated list of features to include in the new window. Table 8.1 shows the features supported by current browsers (version 4.0 and later of Netscape and Internet Explorer).

You can list these attributes in any order, and you need not include them all.

☆ **WARNING** When you type the window method attributes, be sure *not* to type any spaces.

Table 8.1 `window.open()` Method Attributes

Attribute	Value(s)	Description
width	Integer	Allows you to specify the width of the new window's content area apart from any space needed by toolbars and other elements of the window's **chrome** (portions of the window other than the content).
height	Integer	Allows you to specify the height of the new window's content area apart from any space needed by toolbars and other elements of the window's chrome.
left	Integer	Allows you to specify the horizontal position of the left side of the new window. Earlier versions of Netscape 4 did not support this attribute. In practice, versions after 4.77 support it, although Netscape's online documentation suggests using `screenX` instead for Netscape.
top	Integer	Allows you to specify the vertical position of the top side of the new window. Earlier versions of Netscape 4 did not support this attribute. In practice, versions after 4.77 support it, although Netscape's online documentation suggests using `screenY` instead for Netscape.
screenX	Integer	Allows you to specify the horizontal position of the left side of the new window. This attribute works only on Netscape 4 and later browsers.
screenY	Integer	Allows you to specify the vertical position of the top sideof the new window. This attribute works only on Netscape 4 and later browsers.
copyhistory	1 or 0	Transfers the window history (contents of the GO menu) from the old window to the new window.
directories	1 or 0	The Favorites bar in Internet Explorer or the Personal toolbar in Netscape.
location	1 or 0	The Location or Netsite field on top of the browser window that shows the current URL.
menubar	1 or 0	The menu bar at the top of a window in the Microsoft Windows operating system. On the Macintosh, the menu bar is always present, so this attribute is ignored.
resizable	1 or 0	This interface element is usually found in the lower-right corner of the window on Macintosh and Windows. Users can drag it to resize the window.
scrollbars	1 or 0	Allows control over whether the window displays scrollbars.
status	1 or 0	The status bar at the bottom of the window.
toolbar	1 or 0	The toolbar with the Back button found on all browsers.

A new window with all attributes included would require the following statement. The example includes carriage returns for readability. You should be sure to
type it all on one line with *no spaces*.

```
window.open("somepage.html","myWin","width=750,
height=550,left=100,screenX=100,top=50,screenY=50,
copyhistory=0,directories=1,location=1,menubar=0,
resizable=1,scrollbars=1,status=0,toolbar=1");
```

This example creates a window with all features enabled (values set to 1) except
`copyhistory`, `menubar`, and `status` (values set to 0). Both `left/top` and
`screenX/screenY` attributes are included to provide compatibility with all versions of Netscape 4 and Internet Explorer 4 and later browsers.

The only problem with creating a window this way is that you can't easily close
it by using a script. Fortunately, the `open()` method returns a value to identify the
new window. By setting up a global variable, you can store the value and later refer
to it to close the window.

```
var W1 = null;
W1 = window.open("foo.html","myW","width=750,height=550,
scrollbars=1");
```

Later, when you wish to close the window, use the `close()` method of the
window object and reset the variable to null.

```
W1.close();
W1 = null;
```

One of the tedious aspects of creating windows is typing the long list of features and deciding which features are needed. Listing 8.1 solves that problem by
using a function to create a new window called `myWindow`. The function takes
seven parameters. The first two are the URL and the target name. The next four
specify the size and location of the new window. The final parameter contains the
feature set.

There are three prebuilt feature sets. The variable `nofeatures` contains a list
of all the common features, with the values set to 0 to disable them. The variable
`basicfeatures` enables scrollbars, makes the window resizable, and shows the
menu bar (Microsoft Windows only). The variable `morefeatures` enables all the
other features. The variable `dimensions` contains a string specifying the desired
width and height. The variable `placement` contains a long string to indicate the
left and top coordinates in a way that works on all current browsers.

A switch control structure lets you choose the desired feature set. If you pass the
value `none` as the seventh parameter, the `nofeatures` set is used. If you pass the
value basic, the `basicfeatures` set is used. If you pass the value `full`, both the
`basicfeatures` and the `morefeatures`
sets are used. If the value is none of these, the
value is assumed to be a valid text string containing a custom feature set.

☆ **SHORTCUT**   Use Netscape's
JavaScript console (see Chapter
Two) to assist you in debugging
the script.

To begin experimenting with code for managing windows, create the page from Listing 8.1 and load it into a Netscape browser version 4.7 or later.

☆ **TIP**   **Put It in the Library**

Always remember to place reusable scripts in your `mylibrary.js` file. In Listing 8.1, the `openWin()` function will be useful whenever you wish to create a new window and control its size, position, and features.

☆ **TIP**   **Using Switch**

When you want a script to do something depending on the value of a variable, use a switch control structure. It tests the value of a variable or other expression to see whether it matches any of several possible values. When a match is found, specific statements execute; then the `break;` statement tells the switch control structure not to bother testing the other possible cases. If none of the cases is a match, the statements under the word `default` will execute. The switch control structure works in Netscape and Internet Explorer versions 4 and later.

Figure 8.1 shows the output of Listing 8.1.

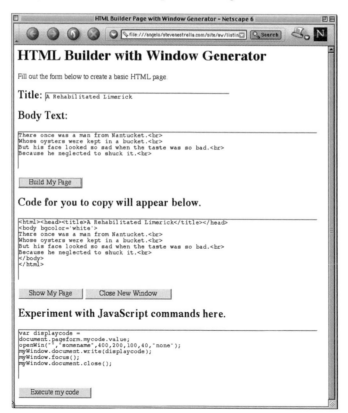

Figure 8.1 Output of Listing 8.1

How Does It Work?

1. The HEAD portion of the page loads into memory. The `mylibrary.js` file loads, a global variable called `myWindow` is created, and three functions are loaded into memory, ready to be called.

2. The BODY loads and displays a form with fields and buttons. The visitor types a title and body text into the first two fields and clicks the button Build My Page. The `buildPage()` function (stored in `mylibrary.js`) is called to assemble a standard HTML page and display the code in the field `mycode`. For more information about the `buildPage()` function, see Chapter Two.

3. The visitor clicks the button Show My Page, which calls the `showPage()` function.

4. The `showPage()` function takes the contents of the `mycode` field and stores it in the new variable `displaycode`. Then the `openWin()` function is called and seven parameters are passed. The first parameter is empty because the document you wish to display is not a preexisting Web page but rather is the output of the code found in the `mycode` field. The second parameter is an arbitrary name, `myPopup`, to serve as the target name. The next four parameters establish the width, height, left coordinate, and top coordinate of the new window. The final parameter passes the value `basic` to indicate that only basic features are requested in the new window.

5. The `openWin()` function receives the seven parameters and stores them in the temporary variables `url`, `targetname`, `W`, `H`, `L`, `T`, and `thefeatures`.

6. A variable called `params` is created to store the text string with all the attributes of the new window. Then the three prebuilt feature sets are defined: `nofeatures`, `basicfeatures`, and `morefeatures`. A variable dimensions and a variable `placement` are created to hold the values for the desired size and location of the new window.

7. A switch control structure chooses the feature set based on the seventh parameter. In this case, the value `basic` was passed, so the contents of the variable `basicfeatures` are added to the contents of the variable `params`.

8. A comma and the values in the variables dimensions and placement are added to the variable `params`. The resulting text string containing in `params` would read

```
scrollbars=1,resizable=1,menubar=1,width=400,
height=200,left=100,top=40,screenX=100,screenY=40
```

9. The `window.open()` method is called to open a new window with the desired feature set. The `window.open()` method returns a value to identify the new window. That value is placed in the global variable `myWindow` created in step 1. Because the `openWin()` function is finished, control returns to the `showPage()` function.

10. The next line of code in `showPage()` after the call to `openWin()` takes the content of the variable `displaycode` and writes it to the document in the new window referred to by the variable `myWindow`. Because the content of the variable `displaycode` is a text string containing standard HTML code, the new window displays a nicely formatted Web page.

11. The `focus()` method of the `window` object is applied to the new window to ensure that it is not hidden behind any other windows.

12. The `close()` method of the document object is applied to the document loaded in the new window to indicate that no further content will be written to the document. However, the `close()` method of the document object does not close the window. It ends the writing session that was begun when the `document.write()` method was applied.

13. The visitor stares appreciatively at the new window, moves it to one side of the screen, clicks back on the main window, and clicks the button Close New Window. The `closeWin()` function is called. It checks to see whether the value in the variable `myWindow` is anything other than null. If it is, it calls the `close()` method of the `window` object. Because that closes the new window, it then makes sense to set the value of `myWindow` to `null` to indicate that the window no longer exists.

14. The visitor notices some sample code in the final text field. The sample code includes a call to `openWin()`. The visitor changes the width and height values in the third and fourth parameters of the `openWin()` function call and changes the seventh parameter from `basic` to `full`.

15. The visitor clicks the button Execute My Code, which calls the `runCode()` function.

16. The `runCode()` function takes the text the visitor altered in the field `codefield` and assigns it to a variable called `thecode`. The `eval()` function then evaluates the contents of `thecode`. Because the contents contain valid JavaScript statements, the code is executed and a new window appears on the screen with the altered feature set and dimensions.

◎◎ Additional Methods of the Window Object

Throughout this book you have made liberal use of the `window.alert()` method to display alert boxes. You have also used the `window.prompt()` method to obtain text input from your visitors. Another useful method of the window object is the `confirm()` method, which displays a dialog box containing any text you pass to it. If the visitor clicks OK, the `confirm()` method returns the value true. If the visitor clicks Cancel, the value returned is false. The returned value can be placed in a variable and tested, as shown in Listing 8.2.

```
<html><head><title>Confirmation</title>
<script type='text/javascript' language='Javascript'>
<!--
var visitorChoice = window.confirm("Are you sure you ¬
want to be here?");
var stuffToWrite = "";
if (visitorChoice){
    stuffToWrite = "It is good to see you can make ¬
decisions.";                 visitorChoice will be
}else{                        true if the visitor clicks OK.
    stuffToWrite = "Too bad.";
}
//-->
</script>
</head>
<body bgcolor='white'>
<p>
<script type='text/javascript' language='Javascript'>
document.write(stuffToWrite);
</script>
</p>
</body>
</html>
```

Listing 8.2 The `window.confirm()` Method

Figure 8.2 shows the output of Listing 8.2.

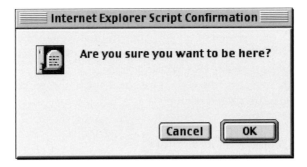

Figure 8.2 Output of Listing 8.2

Another useful feature of the `window` object is the `location` object, which you first encountered in Chapter Five. The `location` object is the URL loaded in the current window. The HREF property of the `location` object contains the entire URL. Changing the HREF property to a different URL causes the window to load a different page. In Listing 8.1, a new window called `myWindow` was created. To change the URL of the new window, you can use a statement such as the following.

```
myWindow.location.href = "someURL.html ";
```

The window object has a useful history object that stores a list of pages recently loaded into the window. To navigate to any of the pages in the list, use the following statement and substitute a positive or negative integer as the parameter.

```
window.history.go(integer);
```

For example, `window.history.go(-3)` would produce a result similar to clicking the Back button three times.

JavaScript and Frames

Frames are common in Web sites both large and small. A typical arrangement consists of a set of two frames (called a **frameset**): a navigation frame on the left, and a content frame on the right. Listing 8.3 creates a set of two frames, called `navigation` and `content`, to assist visitors in viewing the listings from Chapter Two. Listing 8.4 shows the `navbar.html` file that will appear in the navigation frame. Listing 8.5 shows the code for the `home.html` file that is initially loaded in the content frame.

```
<html><head><title>Frameset for Chapter Two</title>
</head>
<frameset cols="150,*">
<frame src="navbar.html" name="navigation">
<frame src="home.html" name="content">
</frameset></html>
```

Listing 8.3 A Frameset for the Examples in Chapter Two

```
<html><head><title>Navigation Bar for Chapter Two
</title></head>
<body bgcolor="aqua">
<h4><a href="home.html" target="content">HOME</a></h4>
<h4><a href="listing2.1.html" target="content">
listing 2.1</a></h4>
<h4><a href="listing2.2.html" target="content">
listing 2.2</a></h4>
<h4><a href="listing2.3.html" target="content">
listing 2.3</a></h4>
<h4><a href="listing2.4.html" target="content">
listing 2.4</a></h4>
<h4><a href="listing2.6.html" target="content">
listing 2.6</a></h4>
<h4><a href="listing2.8.html" target="content">
listing 2.8</a></h4>
<h4><a href="listing2.9.html" target="content">
listing 2.9</a></h4>
</body></html>
```

Listing 8.4 `navbar.html`, the Navigation Frame for the Frameset in Listing 8.3

```
<html><head><title>Frame Scripting</title>
<script type="text/javascript" language="JavaScript">
<!--
function unframeIt(){                    Displays the page without frames.
    if (top.location != self.location){
        top.location.replace(self.location);
    }
}
function frameIt(){                      Displays the page within the frameset.
    if (top.location == self.location){
        top.location.replace("listing8.3.html");
    }
}
//-->
</script>
</head>
<body bgcolor="white">
<p><a href="javascript:unframeIt();">View this page
without frames.</a></p>
<p><a href="javascript:frameIt();">View this page with
frames.</a></p>
</body>
</html>
```

Listing 8.5 `home.html`, the Content Frame for the Frameset in Listing 8.3

Figure 8.3 shows the result of executing Listings 8.3, 8.4, and 8.5.

Frames are best visualized as a hierarchy of multiple window objects in a parent–child relationship. In fact, browsers treat individual frames almost exactly the way they treat windows. The **parent window** in Listing 8.3 contains a document object that merely includes the HTML code to load the frameset. Each of the two **child windows** (Listings 8.4 and 8.5), however, contains a document object that loads standard HTML pages (`navbar.html` and `home.html` in this example) into the left and right frames.

Each window can be referred to as `self` in any script located in the window. The window at the top of the hierarchy can be referred to as `top`. In Listing 8.5, the functions `unframeIt()` and `frameIt()` are called by pseudo-URLs in the two links on the page.

The `unframeIt()` function compares the location of the current window (`self`) to the location of the window at the top of the hierarchy (`top`). If they are not the same, it means that the child window (`self`) is being viewed inside a frameset. To get the child window out of the frameset, the location of the top window (`top`) is replaced with the location of the child window (`self`).

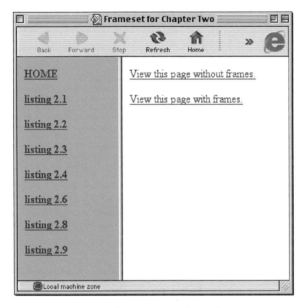

Figure 8.3 Output of Listings 8.3 through 8.5

The `frameIt()` function compares the location of the current window (`self`) to the location of the window at the top of the hierarchy (`top`). If they are the same, it means that the child window (`self`) is not being viewed inside a frameset. To get the child window into the frameset, the location of the top window (`top`) is replaced with the location of the frameset (`listing8.3.html`).

In Listing 8.5, the visitor chooses whether or not to load the page in a frames context. To make that choice for your visitor, you call either function using an `onload` handler in the `BODY` tag. In both functions, the `replace()` method of the `location` object is used so that the reference to the current page in the history is replaced with the reference to the desired page. The alternative is to change the `HREF` property of the location object, as seen in Chapter Five. That works fine in this example, but if these functions are called using an `onload` handler in the `BODY` tag, the `HREF` technique causes problems when the visitor clicks the Back button.

In Listing 8.1 you learned to use the `document.write()` method to display content in another window. Listings 8.6 and 8.7 demonstrate how you can write content dynamically to another frame. Listing 8.6 shows the opening frameset. The file `htmlframebuilder.html` (see Listing 8.7) is loaded into the left frame, `builder`. For the file `blank.html`, you create a simple HTML file with a white background and no text in the body.

```
<html><head><title>Frameset for HTML
Builder</title></head>
<frameset cols="300,*">
    <frame src="htmlframebuilder.html" name="builder">
    <frame src="blank.html"  name="content" >
</frameset>
</html>
```

Listing 8.6 Frameset for a Modified HTML Builder Page

In Listing 8.7 the visitor types information into two fields to enter a title and some text content for a new Web page. The visitor then clicks the button Show My Page, and the `showPage()` function is called. It calls the `buildPage()` function from `mylibrary.js` to assemble the HTML and display it in the `mycode` field. The value in `mycode` is then stored in a variable called `displaycode`. Then `displaycode` is written to the document object contained in the content frame of the parent window (`parent.content.document.write(displaycode)`). Finally, the write session to the content frame is closed. The visitor then sees the new Web page displayed in the content frame, as shown in Figure 8.4.

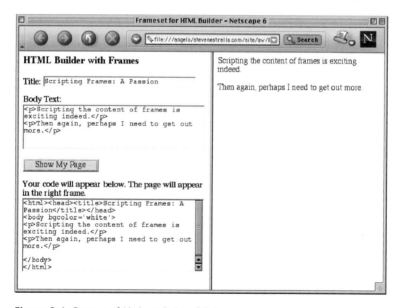

Figure 8.4 Output of Listings 8.6 and 8.7

```html
<html><head><title>HTML Builder Page with Frames</title>
<script type="text/javascript" language="Javascript"
src="mylibrary.js">
</script>
<script type="text/javascript" language="Javascript">
<!--
function showPage(){
    buildPage();
    var displaycode = document.pageform.mycode.value;
    parent.content.document.write(displaycode);
    parent.content.document.close();
}
//-->
</script>
</head>
<body bgcolor="white">
<h3>HTML Builder with Frames</h3>
<form name="pageform">
<p><b>Title:</b> <input type="text" name="pagetitle"
size="35" value="A Basic HTML Page"></p>
<p><b>Body Text:</b><br>
<textarea name="bodytext" cols="40" rows="4">
Replace the text you are reading now with the text of
your choice.
</textarea></p>
<p><input type="button" value="Show My Page"
onclick="showPage();"></p>
<p><b>Your code will appear below. The page will appear
in the right frame.</b><br>
<textarea name="mycode" cols="40" rows="8">
The code will be shown here.
</textarea></p>
</form>
</body>
</html>
```

> You created the buildPage() function in Chapter Two and stored it in mylibrary.js.

Listing 8.7 htmlframebuilder.html, the Builder Frame for Listing 8.6

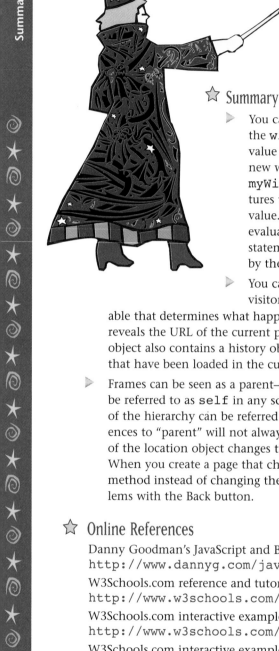

☆ Summary

▷ You can open new windows of any size or position using the `window.open()` method, which returns an ID value that can be stored in a variable. You close the new window through scripting (for example, `myWindow.close()`). You can use switch control structures to implement decision making based on a variable's value. The `eval()` function is built into JavaScript and evaluates whatever text is passed to it. Valid JavaScript statements passed to the `eval()` function are executed by the JavaScript interpreter in the Web browser.

▷ You can use the `window.confirm()` method to query visitors and get a true or false response, storing it in a variable that determines what happens next. The `HREF` property of the location object reveals the URL of the current page; changing `HREF` loads a new page. Each window object also contains a history object. The history object maintains a list of pages that have been loaded in the current window.

▷ Frames can be seen as a parent–child hierarchy of window objects. Each window can be referred to as `self` in any script located in the window; the window at the top of the hierarchy can be referred to as `top`. Because framesets can be nested, references to "parent" will not always be equivalent to "top." The `replace()` method of the location object changes the URL stored in the history index for that page. When you create a page that changes location upon loading, use the `replace()` method instead of changing the `HREF` property. This practice avoids creating problems with the Back button.

☆ Online References

Danny Goodman's JavaScript and Browser Objects Quick Reference
`http://www.dannyg.com/javascript/quickref/index.html`

W3Schools.com reference and tutorial on creating sites with frames
`http://www.w3schools.com/html/html_frames.asp`

W3Schools.com interactive examples of using window method
`http://www.w3schools.com/js/js_window.asp`

W3Schools.com interactive examples of using frames
`http://www.w3schools.com/js/js_frames.asp`

☆ Review Questions

1. Explain the use of `screenX` and `screenY` as opposed to `left` and `top`.

2. Why is it desirable to create a global variable for the name of each new window you create?

3. Explain the default section of a switch control structure.

4. What is the `focus()` method?

5. What is the difference between the HREF property of the `window.location` object and the URL property of the `document` object?

6. Why is parent not always top in the hierarchy of frames?

7. What is `self`?

8. Explain how the `eval()` function can be used in testing code.

9. Given a frameset with a frame on the left called `nav` and a frame on the right called `stuff`, what is the code to add to the document in the `nav` frame to write content to the `stuff` frame?

☆ Hands-On Exercises

1. Make sure you have placed the `var myWindow = null` declaration, the `openWin()` function, and the `closeWin()` function from Listing 8.1 into your `mylibrary.js` file. Create a page that loads mylibrary.js and opens a new window when the visitor clicks a button. The content you load in the new window is up to you.

2. Change the parameters in the code of the previous exercise to create new windows with different sizes, locations, and features.

3. Create a page with a new function that uses the `window.confirm()` method. Create a button that calls your new function. When the visitor clicks the button, confirm that he wishes to close the window. If he confirms, the window closes. Otherwise, the window does not close.

4. Create a variant of the previous exercise. In this version have a new page load in the window if the visitor clicks the Cancel button.

5. Create a frameset with two frames. Create buttons in the left frame that change content in the right frame. Create buttons in the right frame that change content in the left frame. Create a button in either frame that loads different content into each of the two frames.

CHAPTER NINE

APPLIED WEB PROGRAMMING TECHNIQUES

In the previous chapters you learned fundamental concepts about JavaScript and the ways it interacts with the objects in a Web browser. In this chapter you'll see five examples of those concepts in action. You'll learn practical techniques for making your Web pages more useful and compelling.

Chapter Objectives

☆ To learn how to use a triple nested loop to generate an interactive table of Web-safe colors

☆ To discover how to combine JavaScript with client-side image mapping to enhance the user interface of your Web pages

☆ To find out how to detect the visitor's browser and platform

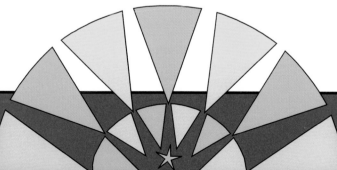

Generating Content with Nested Looping

☆ To understand how to change the text displayed in the visitor's status bar to provide your own content

☆ To learn how to create scrolling text in a text field

☆ To get a glimpse of how Dynamic HTML and Cascading Style Sheets can boost the power of your JavaScript programming

◎◎ Generating Content with Nested Looping

Web developers make esthetic judgments about the background color of each page they create. One way to experiment with background colors is to repeatedly adjust the bgcolor property of the BODY tag in the HTML and then reload the page to see the new color—a tedious process. With a little programming, you can create a highly interactive table that makes it easy to experiment with background colors (see Figure 9.1).

Listing 9.1 creates a standard HTML table and stores it in a variable while the HEAD loads. When the BODY loads, a script writes the content of the variable to the document to create the color table. The trick here is to use a triple nested loop for the red, green, and blue values used in the table.

```
<html><head><title>Web-Safe Colors</title>
<script type="text/javascript" language="JavaScript">
<!--
var safeRGB = new Array('00','33','66','99','cc','ff');
var hexvalue = "";
var tablecontent = "";
tablecontent = "<table width=480 border=0>";
var tdcontent1 = "<td width=80 height=40 bgcolor=#";
var tdcontent2 = " align=center valign=middle>";
var tdcontent3 = "<input type='button' VALUE=";
var tdcontent4 = " onclick='document.bgColor=\"#";
var tdcontent5 = "\"'><\/td>";
for (red=0;red<6;red++){
    for (green=0;green<6;green++){
        tablecontent+="<tr>";
        for (blue=0;blue<6;blue++){
            hexvalue = safeRGB[red] + safeRGB[green] + ¬
safeRGB[blue];
            tablecontent += tdcontent1 + hexvalue + ¬
tdcontent2;
            tablecontent += tdcontent3 + hexvalue + ¬
tdcontent4;
            tablecontent += hexvalue + tdcontent5;
        }
        tablecontent+="<\/tr>";
    }
}
```

This array holds the six hexadecimal values used in the 216 Web-safe colors.

tablecontent holds the entire HTML table. Each cell has a different background color and a button to change the background color of the page.

This triple nested loop generates all the rows and cells of the table.

```
/* After the loop generates all the rows and cells, we
add the closing table tag. */
tablecontent+="<\/table>";
//-->
</script>
</head>
<body bgcolor="white">
<div align="CENTER">
<h1>Chart of 216 Websafe Colors</h1>
<form name="colorform">
<table width="480" border="2">
<tr>
<td align="CENTER" bgcolor="white">
<h3>Click any number to change the background color.
</h3>
<input type="button" value="RESET"
onclick="location.reload();">
</td>
</tr>
</table>
<script type="text/javascript" language="JavaScript">
<!--
document.write(tablecontent);
//-->
</script>
</form>
<p>The following is sample text to assist you in making
judgments about how black text will look on top of
various background colors.</p>
<h6>Sample Level 6 Heading</h6>
<h5>Sample Level 5 Heading</h5>
<h4>Sample Level 4 Heading</h4>
<h3>Sample Level 3 Heading</h3>
<h2>Sample Level 2 Heading</h2>
<h1>Sample Level 1 Heading</h1>
</div>
</body>
</html>
```

Listing 9.1 Preview Table for Web-Safe Colors

Generating Content with Nested Looping

☆WARNING   **Nested Quotes in JavaScript**

When assigning a text string to a variable, you must enclose the text in quotes. If the text itself contains quotes, you can use single quotes for the nested quote. If the text within the nested single quotes requires a quote, however, that quote must be **escaped** (\") using a backslash (\) to ensure that the browser will interpret the quote as part of the desired text string. Otherwise, the quote will prematurely mark the end of the text string and your script won't work. Here, the backslash ensures that the text string assigned to `tdcontent` contains quotes around the hexadecimal color value:

```
var tdcontent = "onclick =
'document.bgColor = \"#FFFFFF\"' ";
```

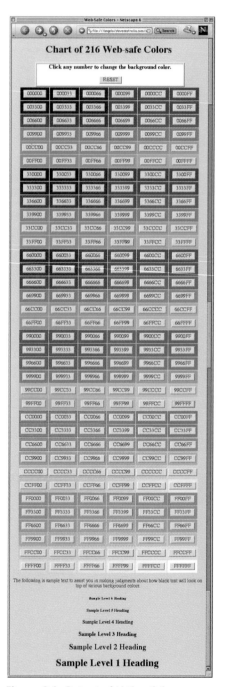

Figure 9.1 Output of Listing 9.1

How Does It Work?

1. The entire content of the SCRIPT tag in the HEAD executes when the page loads.

2. An array is established to hold the six hexadecimal values used in the 216 Web-safe colors. The variable `hexvalue` is created to hold the hexadecimal value to be displayed in each cell of the table. Then the variable `tablecontent` is created to hold all the HTML code that will be used to create the table.

3. Several variables are then initialized to hold the various parts of each table data cell (the `<td>` tag). Each table data cell will display with a different background color and will contain a button; an `onclick` handler will change the background color of the page when the button is clicked. In the forthcoming loop, the parts of each table data cell will be combined with the color value for each cell.

4. A triple nested loop begins, starting with the red values in the outer loop. For each red value, six rows are created. The six rows have the same red value but different green values. The six cells of each row have the same red and green values but different blue values.

5. The elements of the `safeRGB` array are assembled and stored in the variable `hexvalue`. Then the pieces of each table data cell are assembled into the standard code for an HTML table data cell. Here's the string for one of the cells (see "Warning: Nested Quotes in JavaScript"):

```
<td width=80 height=40 bgcolor=#ffcc99 align=center
valign=middle><input type=button value="ffcc99"
onclick='document.bgColor="#ffcc99"'></td>
```

6. Each cell of the table is added to the contents of the variable `tablecontent`. After six cells are created, the code to add a new row is also added. After all the cells are added, the final closing table tag is added and the table is complete.

7. The BODY loads a FORM containing a normal table to display a button that reloads the page when clicked.

8. A SCRIPT in the BODY uses the `document.write()` method to add the table (from the contents of the variable `tablecontent`) to the document. The FORM ends.

9. Text is added at the end of the document to assist the visitor in making judgments about the appropriateness of a given background color when used with black text.

10. The visitor clicks the buttons to experiment with the colors. If she resizes the window in some Netscape browsers, the color table will not be redrawn, but the opening table with the Reset button will continue to be present. When that happens, she clicks the Reset button to restore the table.

◎◎ Combining JavaScript with Client-Side Image Mapping

It's often desirable to use images to create customized interfaces for your Web pages. In your studies of HTML 4, you probably learned how to create a simple **image map**, an image that contains **hot spots** linked to different pages. The term **client-side** means that the coordinates for the hot spots in the image are stored in the HTML code and read by the client software (the browser). Listing 9.2 demonstrates how you can make your image maps even more interactive by adding event handlers and JavaScript functions. In this example, the name of each northern U.S. Rocky Mountain state is displayed when the visitor rolls the mouse over the portion of the image corresponding to the state. When the visitor clicks the image, more detailed information about the state is displayed.

```
<html><head><title>Northern Rocky Mountain States</title>
<script type="text/javascript" language="JavaScript" >
<!--
/* Arrays to hold info about the states. */
var statename = new Array("Wyoming","Idaho","Montana");
var capital = new Array("Cheyenne","Boise","Helena");
var population = new Array("455,975","1,011,986", ¬
"803,655");
var admissionorder = new Array("44th","43rd","41st");
var admissionyear = new Array("1890","1890","1889");

function showStateName(index){
    document.rockies.facts.value = statename[index];
}

function showStateFacts(index){
    var justthefacts = statename[index] + "\n";
    justthefacts += "Population: " + population[index] ¬
+ "\n";
    justthefacts += "Capital: " + capital[index] + "\n";
    justthefacts += "Entered the union in " ¬
+ admissionyear[index];
    justthefacts += " as the " + admissionorder[index] ¬
+ " state.";
    document.rockies.facts.value = justthefacts;
}
//-->
</script>
</head>
<body bgcolor="white">
<div align="CENTER">
<h2>Northern Rocky Mountain States</h2>
<p><b>Roll your mouse over the map to view state
names.</b><br>
```

Retrieves a name from the statename array and displays it in the facts field.

Retrieves information from all the arrays, adds label text and line breaks, and displays it all in the facts field.

```
<b>Click the states to view the facts.</b></p>
<form name="rockies"><img src="images/rockymts.gif"
width="135" height="90" border="0" usemap="#RockiesMap">
<p><textarea name="facts" cols="50" rows="5">
</textarea></p>
</form>
</div>
<map name="RockiesMap">
```

> The image map areas are defined by coordinates.

```
<area shape="POLY" coords="69,83,118,85,121,50,73,45"
href="javascript:showStateFacts(0);" alt="Wyoming"
title="Wyoming" onmouseover="showStateName(0);">
<area shape="POLY"
coords="38,1,27,64,68,71,70,48,57,43,45,5" href=
"javascript:showStateFacts(1);" alt="Idaho" title="Idaho"
onmouseover="showStateName(1);">
```

> When the mouse rolls over a defined area, the onmouseover handler passes a number to the showStateName( ) function.

```
<area shape="POLY" coords="120,47,121,10,46,1,59,44"
href="javascript:showStateFacts(2);" alt="Montana"
title="Montana" onmouseover="showStateName(2);">
</map>
</body>
</html>
```

> When the mouse is clicked on a defined area, the href attribute sends a pseudo-URL that passes a number to the showStateFacts( ) function.

Listing 9.2 JavaScript with Client-Side Image Map

Figure 9.2 shows the output of Listing 9.2.

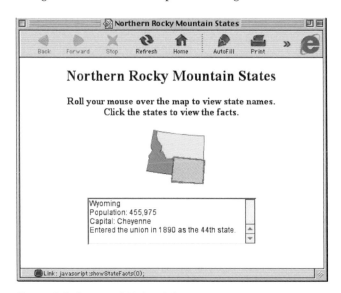

Figure 9.2 Output of Listing 9.2

◎◎ Pseudo-URL versus ONCLICK

Sometimes it's convenient to trigger a JavaScript function or statement when the visitor clicks on a defined area in an image map. There are two ways to do this: the onclick technique and the pseudo-URL technique.

The onclick technique adds an onclick handler to the AREA tag and returns false to prevent the browser from attempting to load the page in the HREF property.

```
<area shape="RECT" coords="0,0,200,300"
href="alternatecontent.html" onclick="myEffect();
return false">
```

Recent browsers (version 4.0 and later) recognize the onclick event handler in AREA tags. A visitor clicks the link, the myEffect() function executes, and false is returned. As a result, the link to alternatecontent.html does not execute, and the visitor remains on the page. But if the same code loads in an older browser, the onclick handler is ignored and alternatecontent.html loads when the link is clicked.

The second technique uses a pseudo-URL. A pseudo-URL has the protocol javascript: in place of the expected http: and tells the browser to execute the statement that follows as JavaScript code. The advantages of this technique are its brevity and its compatibility with older browsers.

```
<area shape="RECT" coords="0,0,200,300"
href="javascript:myEffect();">
```

One small disadvantage of the pseudo-URL technique is that the text javascript:myEffect(); is displayed in the status bar of the window unless you change the status bar text in the myEffect() function. Also, if the function being called returns a value, an error may be generated. To instruct the browser to ignore the returned value, include the void operator:

```
"javascript:void myEffect();"
```

In Listing 9.2, the void operator is not needed because the function does not return a value.

How Does It Work?

1. When the HEAD loads, several arrays are created to hold the factual information about each state.

2. The function showStateName() is created to display the name of a state.

3. The function showStateFacts() is created to display a formatted string of information about the state.

4. The BODY section of the page displays an image of the Northern Rocky Mountain states and an empty text field. The USEMAP property of the IMG tag connects the image to the MAP labeled RockiesMap further down the page.

5. The MAP called RockiesMap defines six areas using coordinates that define the polygons surrounding each state.

6. Each AREA tag contains an onmouseover handler that calls the showStateName() function and passes a number. The showStateName() function looks up the number in the array of state names and displays the appropriate state in the text field.

7. Each AREA tag also contains an HREF property that calls a pseudo-URL. This consists of javascript: and a call to the showStateFacts() function. A number is passed to the function.

8. The showStateFacts() function takes the number it is passed and looks up the necessary information in the various arrays containing factual information about each state. The information is assembled into a text string and displayed in the field.

◎ Detecting the Visitor's Browser and Platform

About 25% of the work that goes into Web development involves testing Web pages on different browsers and platforms and then creating workarounds for any compatibility issues that arise. Some sites even have multiple versions of their opening pages to accommodate different browsers. To determine which page to load, they must first **sniff** (identify) the visitor's browser. Listing 9.3 presents a simple browser sniffer script along with a field and a button. When the button is clicked, the field displays information about the visitor's browser and computer platform.

```
<html><head><title>browser test</title>
<script type="text/javascript" language="JavaScript">
<!--
/* Add this browser detection code to mylibrary.js */
var theApp = navigator.appName.toLowerCase();
```
> theApp will contain the browser name.

```
var UA = navigator.userAgent.toLowerCase();
```
> UA (user agent) contains detailed browser info. For example, UA for Internet Explorer on Mac would be 'mozilla/4.0 (compatible; msie 5.0; mac_powerpc)'.

```
/* variables for the two major browsers in existence
today. */
var isIE = (UA.indexOf('msie') >= 0) ? true : false;
var isNS = (UA.indexOf('mozilla') >= 0) ? true : false;

/* 'compatible' text string exists only in non-Netscape
browsers */
if (UA.indexOf('compatible')>0){
   isNS = false;
}
```

```
/* platform */
var thePlatform = navigator.platform.toLowerCase();
var isMAC = (UA.indexOf('mac') >= 0) ? true : false;
var isWIN = (UA.indexOf('win') >= 0) ? true : false;

/* Most UNIX users use X-Windows so this detects UNIX
most of the time.*/
var isUNIX = (UA.indexOf('x11') >= 0) ? true : false;

/* browser version */
var version = navigator.appVersion;
var isMajor = parseInt( version );
/* Internet Explorer version 5 on the Mac reports itself
as version 4. This code corrects the problem. */
if(isIE && isMAC) {
    if(UA.indexOf("msie 5")) {
        isMajor = 5;
        var stringLoc = UA.indexOf("msie 5");
        version = UA.substring(stringLoc + 5, ¬
stringLoc + 8);
    }
}

/* Netscape 6 reports itself as version 5 on all
platforms. This code corrects the problem. */
if(isNS && isMajor>4) {
    if(UA.indexOf("netscape6")) {
        isMajor = 6;
        var stringLoc = UA.indexOf("netscape6");
        version = UA.substring(stringLoc + 10, ¬
stringLoc + 14);
    }
}
var isMinor = parseFloat( version );

var obsolete = (document.getElementById) ? false : true;
/* End of browser detection code */

function showInfo(){
    var temp="";
    temp += "User Agent: " + UA + "\n";
    temp += "Platform: " + thePlatform + "\n";
    temp += "Macintosh: " + isMAC + "\n";
    temp += "Windows: " + isWIN + "\n";
    temp += "Application: " + theApp + "\n";
    temp += "Version: " + version + "\n";
    temp += "Netscape: " + isNS + "\n";
```

> The variable obsolete is a handy way to encourage visitors to upgrade to a modern browser.

```
    temp += "Internet Explorer: " + isIE + "\n";
    temp += "Major Version: " + isMajor + "\n";
    temp += "Full Version: " + isMinor + "\n";
    temp += "\n";

    if (obsolete){
        temp += "You really should upgrade to a modern ¬
browser.";
        }else{
        temp += "You appear to have a modern browser.";
    }
    document.detectionform.info.value = temp;
}
//-->
</script>
</head>
<body bgcolor="white">
<h1>Browser Information</h1>
<form name="detectionform">
<p><textarea name="info" cols="60"
rows="20"></textarea></p>
<p><input type="BUTTON" name="Show Plugins" value=
"Show Browser Info" onclick="showInfo();"></p>
</form>
</body>
</html>
```

Listing 9.3 Browser Detection

☆ **SHORTCUT**   The sniffer script in Listing 9.3 will come in handy for many uses. It's a good idea to add this reusable code to your `mylibrary.js` file.

☆ **SHORTCUT**   **Learn from the Best**

The browser detection script in Listing 9.3 is based on code made public by Apple Computer on its developer site. Apple's version detects more browsers and provides even more information. One of the great things about working with JavaScript is that an enormous amount of sample code is available online at sites such as `http://developer.apple.com/`, `http://www.builder.com`, and `http://www.javascripts.com`.

Figure 9.3 shows the output of Listing 9.3.

Figure 9.3 Output of Listing 9.3

How Does It Work?

1. The first line of the SCRIPT in the HEAD creates a variable, theApp, to hold a lowercase version of the text string describing the appName property of the navigator object. The navigator object represents the browser. The appName property holds a text string such as Microsoft Internet Explorer or Netscape to describe the browser.

2. The variable UA is created to hold a lowercase version of the text string describing the userAgent property of the navigator object. This property contains identifying information about the browser. The value returned will vary (see "Tip: User Agent Values for Popular Browsers").

3. The variable isIE is created and set to true if UA contains the text string msie. To determine this, the familiar indexOf() method is used.

4. A variable called isNS is created and set to true if UA contains the text string mozilla.

5. Netscape uses the mozilla trade name, but other browsers include the words mozilla and compatible in their userAgent properties. As a result, it is necessary to test for the presence of compatible in UA. If it's found, the browser is not a Netscape browser and isNS is set to false.

6. The variable `thePlatform` is created to hold information about the hardware and operating system in use. The `platform` property of the `navigator` object returns values such as `Win32` (for recent versions of Windows) and `MacPPC` (for recent versions of Macintosh).

7. Variables are established to hold Boolean values that identify the platform and the various versions of popular operating systems. Because of the popularity of the X-Windows graphical browser on the various versions of UNIX, you can test for the UNIX platform by searching for the `x11` string in UA.

8. A `version` variable is created to hold the version number information available in the `appVersion` property of the `navigator` object. The `isMajor` variable is created to hold the integer portion of the version number.

9. Internet Explorer 5 on the Macintosh and Netscape 6 on both platforms report their version numbers incorrectly. As a result, two short conditional structures identify the browser and platform and, if necessary, adjust the version number.

10. The variable `isMinor` holds the full version number.

11. The `obsolete` variable is created to hold a Boolean value that indicates whether the browser is recent. Your viewpoint on what is obsolete may be different. Only a few browsers, such as Netscape 6 and Internet Explorer 5, use the new Document Object Model (DOM1) sanctioned by the World Wide Web consortium. All DOM1 browsers recognize the `getElementById()` method of the `document` object. Those that do not are tagged as obsolete in this code snippet.

12. A function `showInfo()` is created to assemble a text string to report the browser and platform information. The `showInfo()` function is called when the visitor clicks the Show Browser Info button. If the variable `obsolete` evaluates as true, the visitor is cajoled into upgrading his browser.

☆TIP   **User Agent Values for Popular Browsers**

Internet Explorer 5 on Macintosh:
```
mozilla/4.0 (compatible; msie 5.0; mac_powerpc)
```

Internet Explorer 5 on Windows 98:
```
mozilla/4.0 (compatible; msie 5.0; windows 98; digext)
```

Netscape 4.77 on the Macintosh:
```
mozilla/4.77 (macintosh; u; ppc)
```

Netscape 6.1 on Windows:
```
mozilla/5.0 (windows; u; win98; en-us; m18) gecko/20010131
netscape6/6.1
```

◎◎ Controlling Text Displayed in the Status Bar

Web browsers usually have a status bar at the bottom of the window to show the status of the page as it loads and to show a URL when the visitor moves the mouse over a link. One of the earliest uses of JavaScript was to place scrolling text in the status bar. This effect, like the dreaded `<blink>` tag, is now considered tasteless and is rarely used. Sometimes, however, it makes sense to control the text displayed in the status bar. Listing 9.4 demonstrates an easy way to create custom status bar messages that display when the visitor rolls the mouse over your links.

☆**WARNING** Use this effect with care. Text you place in the status bar will override any text the browser wishes to place there. Because the main purpose of the status bar is to allow the browser to communicate with visitors, be sure to make only temporary changes to the text displayed there.

```html
<html><head><title>Status Bar Update</title>
<script type="text/javascript" language="JavaScript">
<!--
var statusText = new Array();
statusText[0] = "";
statusText[1] = "A great place to find scripts for ¬
your pages.";
statusText[2] = "Make your pages come alive with ¬
sound.";
statusText[3] = "More silliness from your favorite ¬
author.";

function statusUpdate(index){
   window.status = statusText[index];
}
//-->
</script>
</head>
<body bgcolor="white">
<p><b>Roll your mouse over the links to see the change
in the status bar.</b></p>
<ul>
<li><a href="http://www.javascripts.com/"
onmouseover="statusUpdate(1);return true;"
onmouseout="statusUpdate(0);return true;">javascripts.com
</a></li>
<li><a href="http://www.beatnik.com/"
onmouseover="statusUpdate(2);return true;"
onmouseout="statusUpdate(0);return true;">beatnik.com
</a></li>
```

> The status property of the window object can be set to any text string.

```
<li><a href="http://www.stevenestrella.com/"
onmouseover="statusUpdate(3);return true;"
onmouseout="statusUpdate(0);return true;">
The Author's Web Site</a></li>
</ul>
</body>
</html>
```

Listing 9.4 Changing Text Displayed in the Status Bar

Figure 9.4 shows the output of Listing 9.4.

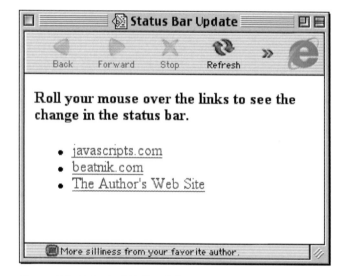

Figure 9.4 Output of Listing 9.4

Using the return true Statement

In the inner workings of standard browsers, a simple link such as

```
<a href="somepage.html">A Link</a>
```

has a built-in response to the mouseover event. When the mouse is rolled over the link, the link becomes active. When a link becomes active, two things happen. First, the content of the HREF property (the URL) is sent to the status property of the window object (window.status). Second, the new status text is displayed in the status bar.

If an onmouseover handler is added to a link, a different sequence of events occurs.

```
<a href="somepage.html"
onmouseover="window.status='stuff';return true;">
A Link</a>
```

Now when the visitor rolls the mouse over the link, the onmouseover handler responds to the mouseover event before the link gets to it. The onmouseover handler calls a function that changes the status property of the window object to "stuff." The built-in behavior of the link that displays the text in the status bar, however, does not occur because the link does not receive the mouseover event. You need the second statement,

```
return true;
```

to get the link to recognize the mouseover event and display the current value of window.status. Otherwise, the status text would be changed but no one would see it because the link would never receive the message to display it.

How Does It Work?

1. An array called statusText is filled with four text strings. The first is blank to clear the status text. The remaining three text strings describe the links on the page.

2. Each link contains onmouseover and onmouseout handlers that intercept the mouseover and mouseout events and call the statusUpdate() function. A number is passed to statusUpdate(), and that number determines which element of the statusText array is assigned to the status property of the window object.

3. The return true statement returns control to the link that responds to the mouseover event by displaying in the status bar the current text found in the window.status property.

◎◎ Scrolling Text in a Text Field

Although scrolling text in the status bar may be tasteless, scrolling text in a text field can be useful. Sometimes you may wish to attract visitors' attention to an important announcement but your design doesn't permit a fancy animation. One way to add interest to your page and gain attention without a lot of multimedia overhead is to use a small text field with scrolling text. Listing 9.5 demonstrates the basic code involved. In this example, the visitor controls the text and its speed. When you create your pages, you'll probably choose to set these parameters yourself.

```
<html><head><title>Scrolling Text</title>
<script type="text/javascript" language="JavaScript">
<!--
var blurb="";
var firstpart="";
var secondpart="";
var delay = 0;
var timerID;
var counter=0;
var scrollstatus="Not Scrolling";
```

Holds the number of the leftmost character in the text string scrolling in the field.

```
function scrollIt(){
    if (scrollstatus == "Scrolling"){
        blurb = document.myform.usertext.value;
        firstpart = blurb.substring(counter, ¬
blurb.length) + " ";
        secondpart = blurb.substring(0,counter);
        document.myform.scrolledtext.value = firstpart + ¬
secondpart;
        (counter > blurb.length) ? counter = 0 : ¬
counter++;
        delay = document.myform.speed.value;
        timerID = setTimeout("scrollIt()",delay);
    }
}
```

When counter reaches the end of the blurb, it starts over at 0. Otherwise, it's incremented by 1.

```
function startScroll(){
    scrollstatus='Scrolling';
    document.myform.scrollfeedback.value = scrollstatus;
    scrollIt();
}
function stopScroll(){
    clearTimeout(timerID);
    scrollstatus='Not Scrolling';
    document.myform.scrollfeedback.value = scrollstatus;
}
//-->
</script></head>
<body bgcolor="white">
<form name="myform">
<h1>Scrolling Text in a Field</h1>
<p>Type the text you want to scroll here.<br>
<input type="text" name="usertext" size="50"></p>
<p>Type delay in milliseconds here.<br>
<input type="text" name="speed" size="10"></p>
<p><input type="BUTTON" onclick="startScroll();"
value="Scroll It!">
<input type="BUTTON" onclick="stopScroll();"
value="Stop This Crazy Thing!">
<input type="RESET" onclick="stopScroll();return true;"
value="Reset All Fields" ></p>
<p>Click the buttons above to control the scrolling text
below.<br>
<input type="text" name="scrolledtext" size="50"></p>
<p>Status<br>
<input type="text" name="scrollfeedback" size="25"></p>
</form>
</body>
</html>
```

Listing 9.5 Scrolling Text Displayed in a Form Field

Scrolling Text in a Text Field

Figure 9.5 shows the output of Listing 9.5.

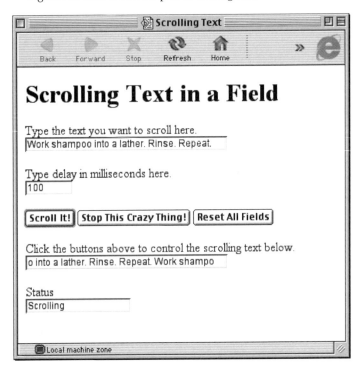

Figure 9.5 Output of Listing 9.5

How Does It Work?

1. The variable `blurb` is created to hold the text the visitor types into the form. The variables `firstpart` and `secondpart` are created to hold the two halves of the blurb as it scrolls. The variable `delay` is created to set the scroll delay between characters. The `timerID` variable is initialized. Later it will be used with the `setTimeout()` method. The variable `counter` is created to track the character number of the leftmost character displayed in the field as the text scrolls. Finally, the variable `scrollstatus` is created to display `scrolling` or `not scrolling` as appropriate.

2. Functions are created to start, maintain, and stop the scrolling.

3. The visitor types a line of text into a text field called `usertext`. The visitor then clicks the button Scroll It! An `onclick` handler calls the `startScroll()` function.

4. The `startScroll()` function sets the `scrollstatus` variable to `Scrolling`, displays `scrollstatus` in the form field `scrollfeedback`, and calls the `scrollIt()` function.

5. The `scrollIt()` function begins by examining `scrollstatus` to see whether the current value is `Scrolling`. If it is, `scrollIt()` places into the variable `blurb` the value the visitor typed. Then a portion (**substring**) of `blurb` is stored in the variable `firstpart`. The first time through the loop, the value of `counter` is 0, so the variable `firstpart` will contain the entire blurb. The fifth time through, however, the value of `counter` will be 4, so `firstpart` will contain characters 4 to the end of `blurb` plus a space. The variable `secondpart` will contain characters 0 to 4.

6. The contents of `firstpart` and `secondpart` are displayed in the field `scrolledtext` on the form called `myform`.

7. A conditional structure checks to see whether `counter` is at the end of the blurb string. If it is, `counter` is reset to 0. Otherwise, `counter` is incremented by 1.

8. The variable `delay` is set to the value typed by the visitor in the field called `speed`.

9. The variable `timerID` is set to an ID number that identifies the scheduled task generated by the `setTimeout()` method.

10. The `setTimeout()` method schedules the `scrollIt()` function to execute again after waiting the number of milliseconds indicated by the variable `delay`. Because `setTimeout()` is calling the function in which it resides, a loop is created.

> ☆ **TIP** A function containing a statement that calls itself is known as a **recursive** function.

11. The visitor clicks the button Stop This Crazy Thing! The `stopScroll()` function is called. The `clearTimeout()` method cancels the next scheduled performance of `scrollIt()`. The variable scrollstatus is set to `Not Scrolling` and displayed in the `scrollfeedback` field.

◎◎ What's Next?

JavaScript is a great tool for adding interactivity to Web pages, but, by itself, it can't do certain things. Among them are the following:

☆ Controlling and animating the location of graphics and text on the screen

☆ Controlling the stacking order of Web page elements to allow objects to overlap

☆ Allowing the visitor to drag objects in a window

☆ Selectively hiding or showing elements in a window

You can create these effects, and many others, using Dynamic HTML.

Dynamic HTML combines HTML version 4, **Cascading Style Sheets (CSS)**, and a scripting language such as JavaScript. If you have recently learned HTML 4, you're familiar with CSS. Cascading Style Sheets level 1, known as CSS1, gives you many formatting options. The current version is CSS2. Internet Explorer 5.5 (IE5.5) and later and Netscape Navigator 6 (NN6) and later fully support CSS1 and most of CSS2. IE4 and NN4 supported some of CSS1 as well as most of the content positioning features of CSS2.

Perhaps the most attractive feature of CSS2 is content positioning. For many years, Web authors have wanted an easy way to have complete control over the position of content. CSS2 lets you position each element precisely on the screen, making the process more efficient than earlier versions. Also, you can indicate the stacking order using the z-index property, allowing overlap of page elements. You can modify the color, size, shape, and position of elements even after the page has loaded. The result is a higher level of interactivity, animation, sound, and video, and even the ability to implement drag-and-drop interfaces. Dynamic HTML takes you and JavaScript to the next level.

Another popular use of JavaScript is to enhance the interactivity possible with products such as Macromedia's Flash, Shockwave, and Dreamweaver, Apple's QuickTime, Adobe's Livemotion and Acrobat, and a host of other programs. These software packages use JavaScript or JavaScript-like languages to offer developers more creative control. As a result, your new skills in JavaScript programming will provide many opportunities to create compelling interactive content.

☆ Summary

▷ You can use a short group of nested loops to create lengthy and complex tables that include background colors and JavaScript code. When you include quotes within quotes within quotes, you may need to escape the most deeply nested quote using the backslash character.

▷ By using client-side image maps with JavaScript, you can create novel and compelling user interfaces that involve substantial interactivity. You can use pseudo-URLs and `onclick` handlers to execute JavaScript code when links and map areas are clicked.

▷ Browser detection is often necessary to deliver different content for different browsers and platforms. Browser detection scripts (sniffers) are ideal candidates for placement in external code libraries such as your `mylibrary.js` file.

▷ You can control the text that is displayed in the status bar of visitors' computers. To avoid interfering with status messages coming from the browser, be sure to place only temporary information in the status bar. An example is a short message that appears when visitors move the mouse over a link.

▷ Scrolling text in a form field is an economical, low-bandwidth way to attract the attention of visitors to important announcements on your page.

▷ Your new skills in JavaScript programming will assist you in creating Dynamic HTML and using authoring environments such as Flash and Director. Dynamic HTML is the combination of JavaScript, HTML 4, and Cascading Style Sheets. Flash and Director are two of many products that use JavaScript or JavaScript-like languages to create interactivity.

☆ Online References

Internet development tutorials and scripts are available at Apple Computer's developer site.
`http://developer.apple.com`

W3Schools.com interactive tutorials contain many useful script ideas.
`http://www.w3schools.com/`

Dr. Estrella's Interactive Web Programming site contains code examples for Dynamic HTML.
`http://www.stevenestrella.com/IWP`

169

☆ Review Questions

1. What are the six hexadecimal values used in all Web-safe colors?

2. When is it necessary to use the backslash to escape a single or double quote character? Give an example.

3. What is a pseudo-URL?

4. What is the `userAgent` property?

5. What is mozilla?

6. How are Boolean values used in browser detection?

7. Which of the major browsers support DOM1?

8. Why must `return true;` be the final statement in an `onmouseover` handler for changing status bar text?

9. What is the easiest way to allow your visitor to blank out all fields on a form and start over?

10. What is a recursive function?

☆ Hands-On Exercises

1. Create a page that uses two nested loops to create content using the `document.write()` method. Then expand the page to include three nested loops.

2. Create a page with a client-side image map and JavaScript code to display text or swap images on the page as the visitor moves the mouse over or clicks on different portions of the image.

3. Create a page that detects the visitor's browser and uses the `window.location.href` property to load different pages for the different browsers.

4. Create a page of links to display different text in the status bar when the visitor rolls the mouse over the links.

5. Create an example of scrolling text in a field. Can you can get the text to scroll backward?

APPENDIX A: ABRIDGED JAVASCRIPT OBJECT REFERENCE

This abridged JavaScript object reference lists the methods, properties, and event handlers most commonly used by those who are new to JavaScript. The list is organized by object and is limited to methods, properties, and event handlers supported by Netscape Navigator and Communicator 4+ and Internet Explorer 4+. At the end of this Appendix you'll find a list of Web addresses that contain more exhaustive online information.

Core JavaScript Objects

Boolean	String		Array	
Methods	Properties	Methods	Properties	Methods
toString()	length	charAt()	length	concat()
valueOf()		charCodeAt()		join()
		indexOf()		reverse()
		split()		sort()
		substring()		
		toLowerCase()		
		toUpperCase()		

Math

Properties	Methods	
E	abs(x)	log(x)
LN2	acos(x)	max(x,y)
LN10	asin(x)	min(x,y)
LOG2E	atan(x)	pow(x,y)
LOG10E	atan2(x,y)	random()
PI	ceil(x)	round(x)
SQRT1_2	cos(x)	sin(x)
SQRT2	exp(x)	sqrt(x)
	floor(x)	tan(x)

Date

Methods

getDate()	getUTCHourc()	setTime()
getDay()	getUTCMinutes()	setYear()
getMonth()	getUTCMonth()	setUTCDate()
getFullYear()	getUTCSeconds()	setUTCDay()
getYear()	getUTCMilliseconds()	setUTCMonth()
getHours()	parse()	setUTCFullYear()
getMinutes()	setDate()	setUTCHour()
getSeconds()	setFullYear()	setUTCMinutes()
getMilliseconds()	setHours()	setUTCSeconds()
getTime()	setMilliseconds()	setUTCMilliseconds()
getTimezoneOffset()	setMinutes()	toGMTString()
getUTCDate()	setMonth()	toLocaleString()
getUTCDay()	setSeconds()	toString()
getUTCFullYear()		

◎◎ Browser Objects

window		document	
Properties	Methods	Properties	Methods
closed	alert()	anchors	close()
document	blur()	applets	getElementById(ID)
event	clearInterval()	body	getElementByName(name)
history	clearTimeout()	cookie	open()
length	close()	domain	write(text)
location	confirm()	forms	writeln(text)
name	focus()	images	
navigator	moveBy()	links	
opener	moveTo()	referrer	
parent	navigate()	title	
screen	open()	URL	
screenLeft	print()		
screenTop	prompt()		
self	resizeBy()		
status	resizeTo()		
top	scroll()		
	scrollBy()		
	scrollTo()		
	setInterval()		
	setTimeout()		

Browser Objects

navigator	img (image)
Properties	Properties
appCodeName	alt
appMinorVersion	height
appName	isMap
appVersion	lowSrc
cookieEnabled	name
cpuClass	src
platform	useMap
userAgent	width

form	
Properties	Methods
action	reset()
elements	submit()
enctype	
length	
method	
name	
target	

input		
Properties	Methods	Event Handlers
checked	blur()	onblur
defaultValue	focus()	onchange
defaultChecked	select()	onclick
disabled	click()	onfocus
form		onmousedown
maxLength		onmouseup

input *(continued)*

Properties	Methods	Event Handlers
name		onselect
readOnly		
size		
src		
tabIndex		
type		
useMap		
value		

select

Properties	Methods	Event Handlers
length	options[index].add()	onchange
multiple	options[index].remove()	
options	blur()	
options[index].defaultSelected	focus()	
options[index].index		
options[index].selected		
options[index].text		
options[index].value		
selectedIndex		
size		
tabIndex		
type		
value		

textarea

Properties	Methods	Event Handlers
accessKey	blur()	onchange
cols	focus()	
defaultValue	select()	
disabled		
form		
name		
readOnly		
rows		
tabIndex		
type		
value		

a (anchor)

Properties	Methods	Event Handlers
href	blur()	onclick
name	focus()	ondoubleclick
tabIndex		onmousedown
target		onmouseout
		onmouseover
		onmouseup

◎◎ Online Reference Materials

ECMA provides a downloadable PDF file of the ECMAScript specification.
`http://www.ecma.ch/ecma1/STAND/ECMA-262.HTM`

Netscape's Online Guide and Reference to JavaScript version 1.5.
`http://developer.netscape.com/docs/manuals/js/core/jsguide15/`
`contents.html`

`http://developer.netscape.com/docs/manuals/js/core/jsref15/`
`contents.html`

W3schools.com provides extensive JavaScript and Dynamic HTML references and
impressive tutorials.
`http://www.w3schools.com/`

The World Wide Web Consortium provides definitive technical specifications on the
Document Object Model.
`http://www.w3.org/DOM/`

APPENDIX B: ANSWERS TO ODD-NUMBERED REVIEW QUESTIONS

Chapter One

1. One example is an image created with the `<img>` tag. It exists as an image object in the browser's memory.

3. Properties have values. The `bgColor` (background color) property of the `document` object, for example, may have a value of `white`, `maroon`, `blue`, or any other valid named color.

5. Here's an example. At a party with five guests, the guests are asked to reveal the most embarrassing moment they ever experienced. In JavaScript, this variable might be called `embarrassingMoment`, and its value will be different for each guest. At the same party, other variables for the guests might include `height`, `weight`, and `age`.

7. Methods are the verbs of the JavaScript language.

9. Boolean values are either true or false.

Chapter Two

1. The assignment operator (=) is used to change the value of the left operand to the value of the right operand. For example, `myFavoriteColor = "maroon"` assigns the value "maroon" to the variable `myFavoriteColor`.

3. JavaScript uses the alert method of the `window` object.

5.
```
if (bookstatus == "open"){
    textvisibility = "true";
}else{
    textvisibility = "false";
}
```

7. The `HEAD` section is completely loaded into the browser's memory before any content in the `BODY` section appears. By placing scripts in the `HEAD`, you're assured that those functions will be available to any event handlers found in the `BODY`.

9. When you place one quoted string within another, alternating single and double quotes assists the Web browser in correctly determining where each text string begins and ends.

Answers

◎◎ Chapter Three

1. If a visitor fails to enter information into a required text field, a validation function can be used to place the pointer in the required field using the `focus()` method.

3. To extract characters from any string objects, the `substring()` method is used.

5. The `length` property can be used to find the number of elements in an array or the number of characters in a `string` object.

7. Consistent, sequential naming of objects makes it possible to use loops effectively.

9. A `SELECT` object on a form has one or more `OPTIONS` associated with it. The `selectedIndex` property contains the number of the option selected by the visitor.

◎◎ Chapter Four

1. The first form always requires the literal name of the image object. The second form lets you use expressions or variables to refer to an image object. The second form is more useful when you're creating functions that will be used with multiple images on a page.

3. Trick question. HTML is *not* case-sensitive today, but you should get in the habit of using all lowercase letters to make your code more compatible with the new version of strict HTML 4.01 known as XHTML. All the following links work equally well today, but the third version is preferred. JavaScript, however, is case-sensitive, so in this example, `swapImage()` should always have an uppercase I.

```
<A HREF = "awl.com"
onMouseOver = "swapImage();">link</A>
<A HREF = "awl.com"
ONMOUSEOVER = "swapImage();">link</A>
<a href = "awl.com"
onmouseover = "swapImage();">link</a>
```

5. The Image object is supported in all browsers that store their images in the `document.images` array. Test for the presence of the array to ensure that only appropriate browsers attempt to run your image swapping code.

```
if (document.images){
    /* code that requires the Image object */
}
```

7. The double rollover technique provides visitors with additional information about a link before they click on the link. This interface enhancement is an impressive and practical way to make navigation easier for your visitors.

◎◎ Chapter Five

1. You must add an `onclick` event handler to call the function.

3. *Parameter* is another word for *variable*. When a function is called, it's possible to send (pass) a value to the function. When the function receives the value, it stores it in a parameter. Statements within the function refer to the value stored in the parameter.

5. The `setTimeout()` method schedules a task for the browser to perform after a given delay. An ID number is assigned to the scheduled task. You use the `clearTimeout()` method to cancel the scheduled task by referring to its ID number.

7. `window.location.href = "http://www.somewebsite.com";`

◎◎ Chapter Six

1. The Web browser is the most common host environment for JavaScript. JavaScript may also be used in other environments. For example, Macromedia Dreamweaver and Adobe Acrobat are computer programs that provide new environments for JavaScript. You can use the skills you learn creating dynamic Web pages to customize the Dreamweaver interface or create workflow procedures in Acrobat.

3. The `getTime()` method of the `Date` object returns the number of milliseconds elapsed since January 1, 1970.

5. The `toLocaleString()` method of the `Date` object returns a formatted text string with the date and time.

7. No. Functions execute their statements only when called. To automatically execute statements in a function, you must create an `onload` handler in the `BODY` tag to call the function after the page finishes loading.

9. The number 6 refers to Saturday.

Chapter Seven

1. A cookie is any piece of data held by an intermediary. The visitor's hard drive is the intermediary between the client and the server.

3. Lou Montulli created the original cookie specification for Netscape Navigator version 1.0.

5. Viruses are computer programs. Cookies are plain text and not computer programs.

7. The `while` loop sets up a condition and continues executing statements until the condition is false. The `for` loop sets up a condition that automatically becomes false after a designated number of times through the loop.

9. The `parseInt()` function takes a text value that begins with a number and returns an integer. This function works when the first character is a numeric value. Because text fields are often used to collect numeric data from visitors, it is often necessary to ensure that the numbers are interpreted as integers rather than text.

Chapter Eight

1. The `screenX`, `screenY`, `left`, and `top` attributes can be used to specify the `left` and `top` coordinates of a window created with the `window.open()` method. `screenX` and `screenY`, however, are supported only by Netscape browsers.

3. If none of the `CASE` statements in a switch control structure contains a match for the value being tested, the statements in the default section will execute.

5. The `HREF` property of the `window.location` object contains the URL of the document loaded in the window. The window may contain any desired URL, so it is possible to change the `HREF` property to a different URL and load a new page. The `URL` property of the `document` object, however, cannot be changed because it represents the location of the document on a Web server. The `document.URL` property, therefore, is read-only.

7. Scripts in a document can refer to the window or frame containing the document as self.

9.
```
parent.stuff.document.write("Anything you wish to
write. ");
parent.stuff.document.close();
```

◎◎ Chapter Nine

1. 00 33 66 99 cc ff

3. JavaScript statements can be triggered in a standard <a></a> tag by including the property `href="javascript:someFunction();"` to call a function when the link is clicked.

5. Netscape Communications uses the trade name mozilla to describe its browsers. Other browsers identify themselves as mozilla-compatible in their `useragent` strings.

7. Microsoft Internet Explorer 5.x and Netscape Communicator 6.x support DOM1.

9. Include the code `<input type="RESET" value="RESET THIS FORM">` to create a standard reset button that works on any form.

INDEX

◎◎ Operators and Control Statements

The following tables present the most commonly used operators and control statements in JavaScript.

Common Arithmetic Operators

Operator	Name	Description
+	Addition	Adds two numbers.
++	Increment	Adds 1 to a variable containing a number.
−	Subtraction	Subtracts one number from another.
−−	Decrement	Subtracts 1 from a variable containing a number.
*	Multiplication	Multiplies two numbers.
/	Division	Divides one number by another.
%	Modulo	Returns the integer remaining after dividing one number by another.

Common Comparison Operators

Operator	Name	Description
==	Equals	Returns true if the operands are equal.
!=	Does Not Equal	Returns true if the operands are not equal.
===	Strictly Equals	Returns true if the operands are equal and of the same type (string, integer, etc.).
!==	Strictly Does Not Equal	Returns true if the operands are not equal and/or not of the same type.
>	Greater than	Returns true if the left operand is greater than the right operand.
>=	Greater than or equal	Returns true if the left operand is greater than or equal to the right operand.
<	Less than	Returns true if the left operand is less than the right operand.
<=	Less than or equal	Returns true if the left operand is less than or equal to the right operand.

Common Assignment Operators

Operator	Name	Description
=	Simple Assignment	Assigns the value on the right side of the expression to the variable on the left (e.g., x = 38).
+=	Compound Assignment Add-by-value	Adds the value on the right side of the expression to the variable on the left and assigns the new value to the variable. For example, if x = 38, then x+=4 would assign the value of 42 to x.
-=	Compound Assignment Subtract-by-value	Subtracts the value on the right side of the expression from the variable on the left and assigns the new value to the variable. For example, if x = 38, then x—=4 would assign the value of 34 to x.
*=	Compound Assignment Multiply-by-value	Multiplies the value on the right side of the expression by the variable on the left and assigns the new value to the variable. For example, if x = 38, then x*=2 would assign the value of 76 to x.
/=	Compound Assignment Divide-by-value	Divides the variable on the left side of the expression by the value on the right and assigns the new value to the variable. For example, if x = 38, then x/=2 would assign the value of 19 to x.
%=	Compound Assignment Modulo-by-value	Divides the variable on the left side of the expression by the value on the right and assigns the remainder to the variable. For example, if x = 17, then x%=3 would assign the value of 2 to x.

Common Logical (Boolean) Operators

Operator	Name	Description
&&	AND	Returns true if both operands are true.
||	OR	Returns true if either of the operands is true.
!	NOT	Returns true if the operand is false.

Operators and Control Statements *(continued)*

Common String Operators

Operator	Name	Description
+	Concatenation	Concatenates (i.e., joins) two text strings.
+=	Concatenate-by-value	Appends additional text to a variable containing a text string.

Common Control Statements

Name	Syntax

if	```if (condition){```
	 ``` statements if condition is true```
	 ```}```

if-else	```if (condition){```
	 ``` statements if condition is true```
	 ```}else{```
	 ``` statements if condition is false```
	 ```}```

? : (conditional operator)	```condition ? expression1 : expression2;```

switch	```switch (expression){```
	 ``` case value1 :```
	 ``` statements if expression equals value1```
	 ``` case value2 :```
	 ``` statements if expression equals value2```
	 ``` case value3 :```
	 ``` statements if expression equals value3```
	 ``` [break]```
	 ``` ...```
	 ``` [default :```
	 ``` statements if expression does not equal```
	 ``` any of the value choices.]```
	 ```}```

for	```for (init. expression; condition; update){```
	 ``` statements```
	 ```}```

while	```while (condition is true){```
	 ``` statements```
	 ```}```